Your Career in Psychology: Clinical and Counseling Psychology

TARA L. KUTHER

Western Connecticut State University

THOMSON

WADSWORTH

Australia • Brazil • Canada • Mexico • Singapore
Spain • United Kingdom • United States

Publisher/Executive Editor: Vicki Knight
Acquisitions Editor: Marianne Taflinger
Editorial Assistant: Lucy Faridany
Marketing Manager: Dory Schaeffer
Marketing Assistant: Laurel Anderson
Marketing Communications Manager: Kelley McAllister
Project Manager, Editorial Production: Marti Paul
Creative Director: Rob Hugel

Art Director: Vernon Boes
Print Buyer: Rebecca Cross
Permissions Editor: Kiely Sisk
Copy Editor: Mary Anne Shahidi
Cover Designer: Roger Knox
Cover Image: Christine Garrigan
Compositor: Brian May
Text and Cover Printer: Webcom

Printed in Canda
1 2 3 4 5 6 7 09 08 07 06 05

Library of Congress Control Number:

2005933249

ISBN 0-534-17480-9

Thomson Higher Education
10 Davis Drive
Belmont, CA 94002-3098
USA

For more information about our products, contact us at:
Thomson Learning Academic Resource Center
1-800-423-0563

For permission to use material from this text or product, submit a request online at
http://www.thomsonrights.com.
Any additional questions about permissions can be submitted by e-mail to

Tara L. Kuther, Ph.D. is Associate Professor of psychology at Western Connecticut State University, where she teaches courses in child, adolescent, and adult development. She values opportunities to conduct collaborative research with students and is active in the Council for Undergraduate Research as Psychology Councilor. Dr. Kuther is Chair of the Instructional Resource Award Task Force of the Office of Teaching Resources in Psychology (OTRP) of the Society for Teaching of Psychology, Division 2 of the American Psychological Association. She has taught both undergraduate and graduate courses at a wide range of institutions, including Lehman College (CUNY), Fordham University, and Teachers College, Columbia University. Her research examines risky behavior during adolescence and young adulthood, moral development, and ethics in research and teaching. She is the author of *The Psychology Major's Handbook,* and coauthor of *Careers in Psychology: Opportunities in a Changing World.* To learn more about Dr. Kuther's research, visit her website at *http://tarakuther.com*

Brief Contents

Chapter 1
Introducing Clinical and Counseling Psychology 1

Chapter 2
Practice Careers   13

Chapter 3
Careers in Public Health and Policy   33

Chapter 4
Psychologists in the Military   51

Chapter 5
Forensic and Police Psychology Careers   63

Chapter 6
Consulting Careers   81

Chapter 7

Psychologists in Academia   97

Chapter 8
Is a Career in Clinical or Counseling
Psychology for You? 113

References   122

Index   128

Contents

Chapter 1
Introducing Clinical and Counseling Psychology 1

Clinical Psychology   2

Counseling Psychology   3

Differentiating Clinical and
Counseling Psychology   4

Other Mental Health Professions   4
    Psychiatrist 5
    Social Worker   5
    Counselor   5

Current Issues in Clinical and
Counseling Psychology 6

Recommended Readings   7

Web Resources 8

Profile 1.1: Elaine M. Heiby, Ph.D.   9

Chapter 2
Practice Careers   13

Activities of Practicing Psychologists   14

Employment Settings   15
    Private Practice   15
    College and University Counseling Centers   16
    Community Mental Health Centers 16
    Hospitals and Medical Centers   16

Advantages and Disadvantages to a Career in Psychological Practice   16

Preparation for a Career in Psychological Practice   18

Recommended Readings   18

Web Resources 19

Profile 2.1: Brick Johnstone, Ph.D.   19

Profile 2.2: Stuart Tentoni, Ph.D.   22

Profile 2.3: Marilu Price Berry, Ph.D.   27

Profile 2.4: Brian R. Snider , Ph.D.   30

Chapter 3
Careers in Public Health and Policy   33

What Is Public Health? 34

Employment Settings   35

Career Tracks   35
    Research   35
    Politics   37
    Program Development and Evaluation   38

Preparation for a Career in Public Health and Social Policy   39

Recommended Readings   39

Web Resources 40

Profile 3.1: Simon H. Budman, Ph.D.   40

Profile 3.3: APA's Congressional and Executive Branch
    Fellowship Program   45

Chapter 4
Psychologists in the Military   51

Activities of Psychologists in the Military 52
    Personnel Selection and Classification   52
    Personnel Training 52
    Leadership and Team Effectiveness 53
    Direct Service   53

Advantages, Disadvantages, and Salary   54

Preparation for a Career in the Military 56

Recommended Readings   58

Web Resources 58

Profile 4.1: Carrie Dorson, Psy.D.   59

Chapter 5
Forensic and Police Psychology Careers   63

Forensic Psychology   64
    Activities of Forensic Psychologists   65
    Advantages and Disadvantages of a Career in Forensic Psychology   67
    Preparation for a Career in Forensic Psychology   68

Police Psychology   68
    Activities of Police Psychologists   68
    Advantages and Disadvantages to a Career in Police Psychology   69

Preparation for a Career in Police Psychology   70

Recommended Readings   70

Web Resources 71

Profile 5.1: Karen Franklin, Ph.D.   72

Profile 5.2: Evan Nelson   74

Profile 5.3: Ellen Kirchman, Ph.D.   77

Profile 5.4: Gary Kaufmann, Psy.D.   78

Chapter 6
Consulting Careers 81

Management Consultant   82
 Advantages and Disadvantages of a Career as a
 Management Consultant   83
 Preparing for a Career as a Management Consultant 83

Executive Coach   84

Activities and Professional Responsibilities. What Do Executive Coaches Do?
          84
 Advantages and Disadvantages to a Career as an Executive Coach   85

Preparation for a Career as an Executive Coach   86

Recommended Readings   87

Web Resources 88

Profile 6.1: Steven Williams, Ph.D., S.P.H.R.   88

Profile 6.2: More Psychologists Are Attracted to the
          Executive Coaching Field   91

What it is   92

What it takes   93

Ways to sample the field   94

Chapter 7
Psychologists in Academia 97

A Career as a Professor 98
 Activities and Professional Responsibilities   98
 Advantages and Disadvantages to a Career as a Professor   100

A Career in Research   102
 Academia   102
 Industry   103
 Government   103

Social Service Agencies and Nonprofits   104
Preparation for a Teaching and Research Career   104

Recommended Readings   105

Web Resources 105

Profile 7.1: Richard M. McFall, Ph.D.   106

Profile 7.2: Peter J. Snyder, Ph.D.   109

Chapter 8
Is a Career in Clinical or
Counseling Psychology for You?   *113*

Master's Degrees in Clinical and Counseling Psychology   114
What Can You Do with a Master's Degree?   114
What Does a Master's Degree Entail?   115

Doctoral Degrees   115
Training Models   115
Ph.D. vs Psy.D.   116
What Does a Doctoral Degree Entail?   117
Post-Doctoral Specialization 118

Licensure   118

Advancing Your Career: What You Can Do Now   119
Become Known by Your Professors   120
Obtain Research Experience   120
Obtain Applied Experience 120
Begin Preparing for Graduate Study 121

Recommended Readings   121

Web Resources 121

References   *122*

Index *128*

References   122

Index 128

Preface

Did you know that slightly more than one-half of all doctoral degrees in psychology are conferred within the subfields of clinical and counseling psychology? Most students who consider graduate study in clinical or counseling psychology are familiar with practice-related careers; however, applied psychologists have many more career options available to them than many students (and often psychologists themselves) realize.

My goal in writing *Your Career in Psychology: Clinical and Counseling Psychology* is to introduce students to the variety of career opportunities available. Each chapter presents a career path, including an overview, advantages and disadvantages, and a profile of psychologists who have chosen that path. Consider this book a starting point for exploring careers in clinical and counseling psychology. Discuss the career opportunities you find within these pages with your advisor and psychology professors and explore the resources provided at the end of each chapter for further information on the specific fields and careers.

Your Career in Psychology: Clinical and Counseling Psychology begins by discussing the nature of clinical and counseling psychology, distinguishing them from other mental health professions. Chapter 2 explores practice-related careers in a variety of settings, from private practice to medical centers. Opportunities in public health and policy are presented in Chapter 3; many psychologists affect change through their policy-oriented research, political work, and program development and evaluation, rather than through the one-on-one therapeutic work that we ordinarily envision. Clinical and counseling psychologists hold important roles within the military; Chapter 4 discusses military careers for psychologists. Psychology also holds many implications for understanding the criminal mind and aiding the legal system. In Chapter 5, we examine careers in forensic and police psychology. Some clinical and counseling psychologists find careers in business settings, via consulting, as discussed in Chapter 6. Although most students are familiar with the roles of psychology professors, they may not be aware of the many activities in which professors en-gage; Chapter 7 covers academic careers. The final chapter of *Your Career in Psychology: Clinical and Counseling Psychology* explores graduate training in these applied areas, master's and doctoral degrees, licensure, postdoctoral spe-cialization, and what you can do now to advance your career in psychology.

Acknowledgements

I thank Marianne Taflinger for taking this project under her wing, guiding it through the review and revision process, and sharing her expertise. Thanks to Vicki Knight for identifying the promise of this project and directing it to the appropriate channels to make it happen. Margarita Posada provided feedback and helpful suggestions that improved the quality of each chapter within this book. Thanks to Mary Anne Shahidi for her copyediting expertise. Finally, I thank my parents, Philip and Irene Kuther, for their unwavering support through the years.

INTRODUCING CLINICAL AND COUNSELING PSYCHOLOGY

CHAPTER GUIDE

CLINICAL PSYCHOLOGY

COUNSELING PSYCHOLOGY

DIFFERENTIATING CLINICAL AND COUNSELING PSYCHOLOGY

OTHER MENTAL HEALTH PROFESSIONS

PSYCHIATRIST

SOCIAL WORKER

COUNSELOR

CURRENT ISSUES IN CLINICAL AND COUNSELING PSYCHOLOGY

RECOMMENDED READINGS

WEB RESOURCES

PROFILE 1.1: ELAINE M. HEIBY, PH.D.

Clinical and counseling psychology, the predominant areas of psychological practice, are familiar to most students, because psychologists are portrayed often in television shows, films, and other media. Talk shows, like *Oprah, Ricki Lake*, and *Dr. Phil*, depict psychologists providing insight into interpersonal problems among families, couples, and friends. Psychologists write magazine articles and popular books, like *Emotional Intelligence at Work* and *Awakening at Midlife*, to help us learn more about ourselves and how to successfully navigate our lives. Given the widespread attention to the practice areas of psychology, and our inherent interest in understanding what makes people tick, as well as the desire to help others, it's not surprising that clinical and counseling psychology are very popular areas of study. For example, of the 4,700 doctoral degrees in psychology conferred during the 2000–2001 school year, 53%, or 2,476, were in the subfields of clinical and counseling psychology (National Center for Education Statistics, 2003). Despite widespread awareness of psychological practice, many misconceptions persist about the functions and roles of clinical and counseling psychologists. The fields of clinical and counseling psychology share many similarities, so it's not unusual for students to find it difficult to differentiate the two. In this chapter, we discuss clinical and counseling psychology, and explore their distinctions, as well as related mental health disciplines that are similarly misunderstood.

CLINICAL PSYCHOLOGY

Clinical psychology is the largest subfield of psychology, with 2,183 doctoral degrees and 1,820 master's degrees conferred in 2000–2001 (National Center for Education Statistics, 2003). Clinical psychology is the study of emotional, behavioral, and psychological disorders, including their causes, diagnoses, and treatment. Clinical psychologists apply research-based knowledge to predict, assess, explain, and alleviate psychological problems and distress in people of all ages (Society of Clinical Psychology, 2002).

You're probably familiar with the practitioner role of the psychologist from watching movies like *What About Bob?* and *Analyze This*. In practice settings, clinical psychologists assess and treat people who are experiencing psychological problems and disorders that may range from normative difficulties, such as grief after losing a loved one or anxiety after being victimized by crime, to more serious and chronic disorders, such as schizophrenia, major depression, or bipolar disorder. Some clinical psychologists specialize in particular populations, like children or older adults, or specific problems, like depression or eating disorders. Other clinical psychologists work as generalists, dealing with all ages and all types of problems. Clinical psychologists also conduct research. For example, some devise new assessment techniques for identifying persons suffering from psychological disorders. Others study the effectiveness of various forms of treatment for psychological disorders, such as new therapeutic techniques, medication, or behavioral management programs.

Clinical psychologists practice, conduct research, teach, engage in program development and evaluation, and work as supervisors and administrators in health care settings such as hospitals, mental health centers, and private practice, as well as in settings outside of health care, including universities, government, business, and more. We'll take a closer look at each of these activities, and the settings in which they occur, throughout this book.

COUNSELING PSYCHOLOGY

With 5,413 master's and 293 doctoral degrees awarded during the 2000–2001 school year (National Center for Education Statistics, 2003), counseling psychology runs a close second in popularity to clinical psychology. Counseling psychology emphasizes the study of normative functioning and growth, rather than psychological distress. Counseling psychologists study and work with people suffering from emotional, behavioral, and psychological disorders; however, counseling psychologists focus on promoting overall functioning, rather than treating pathology.

Counseling psychologists study how to foster individual development and maximize skills, interests, and abilities to promote individual growth. They conduct therapy to help people adjust to everyday life issues and changes, such as marriage, career change, childbirth, and transitions to and from college. Counseling psychologists also conduct vocational assessments and provide career guidance to help individuals select careers that match their interests and abilities.

In research settings, counseling psychologists study how to promote healthy functioning and adaptive growth. For example, a counseling psychologist might examine how people cope with daily hassles and how different coping strategies fare in helping people adapt. Or a counseling psychologist might create and test an assessment tool to help people choose careers that match their interests and skills. Counseling psychologists practice, conduct research, teach, develop and evaluate programs, and work as supervisors and administrators in community settings such as mental health clinics, halfway houses, college counseling centers, and social service agencies, as well as in health care settings, universities, government, business, and private practice.

DIFFERENTIATING CLINICAL AND COUNSELING PSYCHOLOGY

A Clinical and counseling psychologists engage in similar activities, including practice, research, teaching, consultation, and administration, and there is much overlap between the two fields. However, despite their similarities, clinical and counseling psychology have different roots and different philosophies of practice.

Generally speaking, clinical psychologists engage in a greater range of activities with a more broad population of clients than do counseling psychologists. Counseling psychologists limit their study and practice to helping people solve problems related to everyday life, including marital problems, difficult transitions, and other personal problems that most of us are likely to experience. Clinical psychologists address all of these functions, and also help people who are experiencing more severe mental illnesses. Traditionally, clinical psychologists study and treat pathology, whereas counseling psychologists emphasize normative functioning and the promotion of assets and strengths though brief interventions (i.e., provide short-term therapy in fewer than 15 sessions) (Gelso & Fretz, 2001; Norcross, 2000). Counseling psychologists are more likely to conduct educational and occupational testing and are found more often in educational settings like colleges and universities than are clinical psychologists (Bechtoldt, Norcross, Wyckoff, Pokrywa, & Campbell, 2001). Of course, you will also find counseling psychologists in the same settings as clinical psychologists—hospitals, rehabilitation centers, mental health clinics, and industry (Trull & Phares, 2001).

Clinical and counseling psychology have different roots, but the distinctions between the two have blurred (Keith-Spiegel & Wiederman, 2000; Norcross, 2000). Clinical and counseling psychologists complete 5 to 7 years of graduate education and internships after acquiring their bachelor's degrees. Clinical and counseling psychologists complete similar graduate programs, typically emphasizing the importance of research and practice, with similarities in coursework (e.g., approaches to treatment, cognitive-behavioral interventions, and supervised practica). Graduates of clinical and counseling psychology programs are eligible for the same professional benefits such as licensure, independent practice, and insurance reimbursement.

OTHER MENTAL HEALTH PROFESSIONS

Clinical and counseling psychologists are not the only mental health-related career fields oriented toward helping people. Because it's easy to confuse the careers of psychiatrists, counselors, and social workers with psychologists, it's worth taking a moment to examine these related mental health fields.

Psychiatrist

A psychiatrist is a physician who specializes in psychiatry. He or she earned a medical degree (M.D.) after 4 years of medical school, and then completed a 3 to 4 year residency program in psychiatry. It is during the residency period that physicians specialize; those who choose to become psychiatrists learn how to diagnose and treat mental illness. Psychiatrists tend to work with clients with serious psychological disorders with biological bases, like schizophrenia. They are trained in emergency and crisis evaluations, inpatient and outpatient treatment, and medication. Because of their medical training, psychiatrists often treat psychological disorders and mental illnesses by prescribing medication; in most states, they are the only mental health professionals who can prescribe medications.

Social Worker

Social workers help people to adapt and function in their everyday environments by providing counseling and identifying needed resources, such as housing, food stamps, and health care. A master's degree in social work requires 2 to 3 years of study (including training in human growth and development, social policies and programs, methods of practice, and social research) and a supervised internship of at least 900 hours of fieldwork. The master's degree in social work (M.S.W.) prepares graduates for service provider careers in hospitals, clinics, schools, correctional facilities, nonprofit agencies, and private practice (Actkinson, 2000). The M.S.W. allows degree-holders to practice therapy independently; social workers are eligible for licensure or certification in all fifty states and the District of Columbia (Bureau of Labor Statistics, 2002).

Counselor

There are many different kinds of counselors (e.g., guidance counselor, career counselor, alcohol and drug abuse counselor), but all work to help people who are experiencing problems or who need assistance in making decisions. For example, school or guidance counselors help students to evaluate their abilities and interests so that they can develop educational and vocational goals that are realistic and achievable. An employment counselor helps people to make career decisions and assists clients with aptitude testing, resume writing, and interviewing skills. An alcohol and drug abuse counselor assists clients in understanding their substance use patterns and overcoming addiction. Counselors work in a variety of settings, including schools, colleges, clinics, social agencies, correctional institutions, drug and alcohol rehabilitation centers, and private practice.

A master's degree in counseling entails 2 years of coursework and an internship of 700–900 hours, depending on state and graduate training. The master's degree in counseling enables graduates to seek licensure and practice therapy independently (varying by state). In 2001, 46 states and the District of Columbia had some form of required credentialing, licensure, or certification of counselors (Bureau of Labor Statistics, 2002). The exact requirements for independent practice vary by state (visit the National Board of Certified Counselors and Affiliates Web site at http://www.nbcc.org to learn about the counselor credentialing requirements in your state).

CURRENT ISSUES IN CLINICAL AND COUNSELING PSYCHOLOGY

The movement toward managed care, in which insurance companies are more selective about who will receive treatment and what treatments will be reimbursed, is changing the nature of psychological practice. The traditional fee-for-service mental health care system offered insurance companies "little control over which doctoral-level practitioners could be used, the amount paid for services, the quality of services, and the frequency of service utilizations" by patients (Trull & Phares, 2001, p. 68). Today's managed care organizations emphasize cost containment, which has implications for psychologists' career opportunities. In one study of nearly 16,000 licensed psychologists, four out of five reported a negative impact of managed care on their practices (Phelps, Eisman, & Kohout, 1998). Doctoral-level psychologists are now "being underbid by master's-level social workers, marriage and family counselors, and psychological assistants, and will be increasingly supplanted in the role of psychotherapist by these master's level professionals" (Humphreys, 1996, p. 190). Costs for master's level professionals are lower and are therefore more attractive to managed care companies (Cummings, 1995).

Humphreys (1996) warns that psychologists will experience what has already happened in psychiatry: "Psychiatrists are still involved in psychotherapy, [but] their role has become circumscribed… Cost-conscious payers prefer not to pay psychiatrist's fees for anything other than what only a psychiatrist can do … such as brief diagnostic assessment and prescription of medications" (p. 192). Some argue that the marginalization of psychologists has begun because the market for independent practitioners (i.e., private practice) is shrinking as solo practice is becoming economically unfeasible; alternatively, group practices are on the rise (Cummings, 1995; Hersch, 1995; Nickelson, 1995).

A second issue that is germane to clinical and counseling psychologists to-day is whether prescriptive authority should be extended to practicing psy-chologists. Traditionally, prescriptive authority for mental health professionals was limited to physicians and psychiatric nurses. However, the American Psy-chological Association has advocated for extension of prescriptive authority to psychologists (APA Practice Directorate, 2002). This issue is hotly debated among psychologists and other health care professionals (Williams, 2000). Ad-vocates for prescription privileges argue that such authority will allow "psy-chologists to provide a wider range of services to a wider range of patients" (Nickelson, 1995, p. 368) and will fill in the gap in services left by the decline in psychiatrists. Since 1970, the proportion of physicians who choose psychi-atric residencies has declined (Sierles & Taylor, 1995). For example, in 1994, only 3% of physicians chose psychiatric residencies, which was the lowest since 1929 (Sierles & Taylor, 1995). The paucity of psychiatrists has left some states without adequate mental health services, like New Mexico, which is the first state to offer psychologists prescription privileges (APA Practice Directorate, 2002), the ability to prescribe psychotropic medications to clients independent of psychiatrists or physicians. In the coming years, the face of psychological practice is likely to change, as several states are considering similar legislation.

Don't be discouraged by these dire warnings. They are not meant to frighten you away from a career in clinical or counseling psychology. Psycho-logical practice isn't ending; instead, it's transforming. Clinical and counseling psychologists must adapt by expanding beyond direct service to program de-velopment, health promotion activities, community intervention, and public advocacy (Himelein, 1999; Humphreys, 1996). Throughout this book, we'll dis-cuss traditional and emerging roles for psychologists.

RECOMMENDED READINGS

Brown, S. D., & Lent, R. W. (Eds.) (2000) . *Handbook of counseling psychology* (3rd ed.). New York: Wiley.

Collison, B. B., & Garfield, N. J. (1996). *Careers in counseling and human services.* New York: Taylor & Francis.

Feldman, S. (2003). *Managed behavioral health services: Perspectives and practice.* Springfield, IL: Charles C. Thomas.

Gelso, C., & Fretz, B. (2001). *Counseling psychology* (2nd ed.). Orlando: Harcourt.

Ginsberg, L. H. (2000). *Careers in Social Work. Saddle River, NJ:* Allyn & Bacon.

Hayes, S. C., & Heiby, E. M. (1998). *Prescription privileges for psychologists: A critical appraisal.* Reno, NV: Context Press.

Kuther, T. L., & Morgan, R. D. (2004). *Careers in Psychology: Opportunities in a changing world.* Belmont, CA: Wadsworth.

Mechanic, D. (1998). *Mental health and social policy: The emergence of managed care.* Saddle River, NJ: Allyn & Bacon.

Norfleet, M. A. (2002). Responding to society's needs: Prescription privileges for psychologists. *Journal of Clinical Psychology, 58,* 599-610.

Srebalus, D. J., & Brown, D. (2000). *Guide to the helping professions.* Saddle River, NJ: Allyn & Bacon

Woody, R. H., & Robertson, M. H. (1997). *A Career in clinical psychology: From training to employment.* Madison, CT: International Universities Press.

WEB RESOURCES

Clinical Versus Counseling Psychology: What's the Diff?
    http://www.psichi.org/pubs/articles/article_73.asp

Counseling Psychology: FAQs
    http://www.counselingpsychology.net/cpfaq.html#maphd

Counseling Psychology: Making Lives Better
    http://www.psichi.org/pubs/articles/article_97.asp

Frequently Asked Questions About Clinical Psychology
    http://www.psych.ucalgary.ca/Clinical/faq.html

Information for Future Practitioners (from APA)
    http://www.apa.org/apags/profdev/practiti.html

Pathways to Helping Professions: Graduate Study in Clinical Psychology and Related Fields
    http://departments.bloomu.edu/psych/pathwaysmain.htm

Social Work Careers
    http://www.collegeview.com/career/careersearch/job_profiles/human/sw.html

Society of Clinical Psychology (APA Division 12)
    http://www.apa.org/divisions/div12/

Society of Counseling Psychology (APA Division 17)
    http://www.div17.org/

PROFILE 1.1: ELAINE M. HEIBY, PH.D.

Dr. Heiby is a Professor of Psychology at the University of Hawaii. Her research interests include theories of self-control, emotional disorders, and adherence to health behaviors, and she has published extensively in these areas. Dr. Heiby is also known for her leadership among those who oppose seeking prescription privileges for psychologists. We had a chance to ask Dr. Heiby about her own background as well as her views regarding prescription privileges.

What originally got you interested in the field of clinical psychology?

When I entered graduate school in 1974, I intended to become an academic in a behavioral psychology program. This was an exciting time in behavioral psychology when the works of scientists like Wolpe, Staats, and Skinner were demonstrating the generalizability of basic laboratory principles to the understanding of complex human behavior and the alleviation of human suffering. I realized I wanted to contribute to the synthesis of behavioral principles and applied psychology. I also understood that clinical psychology was a growing profession with frighteningly few scientifically based guidelines for the selection of effective prevention and treatment programming. So, I chose to complete doctoral training in both clinical and behavioral psychology, knowing that clinical training was essential to being able to concentrate my career on the integration of psychological science and practice.

Describe what activities you are involved in as a clinical psychologist.

I'm a professor in the Department of Psychology at the University of Hawaii at Manoa and am licensed. I teach two psychological assessment courses in our clinical program, serve as the Associate Director of Clinical Studies, supervise graduate and undergraduate clinical research, conduct several of my own research programs, and participate on the boards of organizations of psychologists. I had a small part-time psychotherapy practice for about 10 years. Now my applied work is limited to consultations and serving as an expert witness. Consultations have included developing assessment and treatment protocols for behavioral health providers, conducting treatment outcome evaluations in mental health settings, and providing psychological assessments for family and criminal courts.

What are your particular areas of expertise or interest?

My interests include (a) developing integrative theories of self-control, emotional disorders (depression, anxiety, anger and mania), and adherence to health behaviors; (b) construction of brief assessment devices, including measures of self-control and self reinforcement skills and other behavioral competencies relevant to emotional disorders and adherence to health behaviors; and (c) applying chaos theory to the understanding of fitful and transitional states.

What future trends do you see for clinical psychology?

I find this to be a very exciting time for clinical science and scientist practitioners. The health care environment now requires evidence of cost-effective services. These market demands are congruent with the basic tenets of science that involve pursuit of parsimony and empirical support for predictions. Managed care can be rewarding for the scientist-practitioner whose approach involves the value that scientifically supported services are the most humane ones. Applied psychologists will be needed to train therapists in the most effective procedures, conduct prevention program and treatment outcome evaluations, provide direct services for the more difficult cases, and consult with medical providers, government agencies, businesses, and other organizations. Clinical scientists will find more grant monies to support research on the development of cost effective assessment devices and treatment procedures. So I think that in the future, the scientifically trained clinical psychologists will find the most job opportunities and be the most satisfied with their work.

You have been an outspoken critic of the movement and seek and obtain prescription privileges for clinical psychologists. Why?

I believe psychology's plate is full. There are many unmet societal needs for effective psychological services. Psychologists are the only mental health service providers trained in the science of human behavior and positioned to make the most informed clinical decisions. Researches have barely scraped the surface in understanding the psychological level of human adjustment and suffering. For psychology to take on the task of medical training and practice, something else will have to give. At the training level, the undergraduate psychology major will include premedical courses that will probably not draw many of the students currently interested in the discipline. The graduate training would also be overhauled. Adding several years of medical training to clinical programs would necessarily have to come at the expense of psychology training. Applied psychologists would be less expert in the science of behavior, and there would be fewer psychology faculty conducting both basic and applied research.

Nevertheless, I believe there have been some positive effects of the prescription privileges proposal. Applied psychologists are being encouraged to become more competent in making recommendations to physicians and in evaluating the effectiveness of medical treatment. Researchers are being encouraged to synthesize clinical psychology and behavioral neuroscience. Greater collaboration and integrative research undoubtedly will promote comprehensive services and advance the science of psychology. In the long term, these changes may result in a hybrid discipline and profession that involves the current domains of psychological and medical services. At this point in time, however, I believe the attempt to legislatively transform psychology into a medical specialty is premature. Psychologists who want prescription privileges are free to seek training that is already available, such as in nursing, without reallocating resources away from psychology.

(reprinted with permission from Trull & Phares, 2001)

PRACTICE CAREERS

CHAPTER GUIDE

ACTIVITIES OF PRACTICING PSYCHOLOGISTS

EMPLOYMENT SETTINGS
PRIVATE PRACTICE
COLLEGE AND UNIVERSITY COUNSELING CENTERS
COMMUNITY MENTAL HEALTH CENTERS
HOSPITALS AND MEDICAL CENTERS

ADVANTAGES AND DISADVANTAGES TO A CAREER IN PSYCHOLOGICAL PRACTICE

PREPARATION FOR A CAREER IN PSYCHOLOGICAL PRACTICE

RECOMMENDED READINGS

WEB RESOURCES

PROFILE 2.1: BRICK JOHNSTONE, PH.D.

PROFILE 2.2: STUART TENTONI, PH.D.

PROFILE 2.3: MARILU PRICE BERRY, PH.D.

PROFILE 2.4: BRIAN R. SNIDER, PH.D.

When most people think of a psychologist, the practitioner comes to mind. There's a reason for that: About 60% of clinical and counseling psychologists are employed in practice settings (Gelso & Fretz, 2001; Trull & Phares 2001). Surveys of clinical psychology students indicate that most plan to spend the majority of their professional time in practice (Parker & Detterman, 1988). Also, psychologists engage in multiple roles, so it's not uncommon for psychologists who work in academic and industry settings to engage in practice activities on a part-time basis. For example, one study of clinical psychology faculty members indicated that over one-half of the professors surveyed engaged in practice activities in addition to their academic work (Himelein & Putnam, 2001). In this chapter, we examine careers in psychological practice.

ACTIVITIES OF PRACTICING PSYCHOLOGISTS

Practicing psychologists engage in a variety of activities. Therapy is the most frequent activity of practicing psychologists (Trull & Phares, 2001). Therapy, itself, is diverse in that clients may be children, adolescents, adults, couples, or groups. Clinicians may also specialize in working with a particular type of client (e.g., adolescents) or a particular problem or issue, such as eating disorders, marital difficulties, or substance abuse. In addition to one-on-one work with a client or couple, some therapists also facilitate psychoeducational and psychotherapy groups—groups of people who are experiencing similar problems or who have similar needs and seek therapy together. Regardless of type of client or specialty, practicing psychologists listen to their clients and attempt to understand the problems or challenges and help them learn new ways of coping. There are many styles of therapy and clinicians vary in their styles based on their training and theoretical orientation. For example, therapists with a cognitive behavioral orientation help clients become aware of their thought patterns and learn new ways of thinking and behaving. Therapists who adopt the humanistic approach help clients feel accepted and promote self actualization.

All practicing psychologists engage in some assessment. Assessment occurs through observation, testing, and interviewing. It's a way of gathering information about a client and his or her particular needs. Assessment is a critical part of the practicing psychologist's role and is used to gather the information needed to make a diagnosis and recommendations for treatment. Psychological testing is a major part of the work of practicing psychologists (Young & Weishaar, 1997). Psychologists administer and interpret a variety of personality, neuropsychological, intelligence, and vocational tests.

Psychologists who choose careers in practice often engage in clinical supervision, a type of teaching in which they supervise and train psychology students, interns, master's-level clinicians, and new psychologists who have not yet attained licensure. Supervision entails helping other therapists to become more skilled by discussing their cases and treatment approaches (Young & Weishaar, 1997). Relatedly, "practitioners also provide consultation to other therapists on an as-needed basis to offer a second opinion about a diagnosis, respond to a specific assessment question, help resolve an issue in a therapeutic relationship, or recommend an alternative treatment intervention" (Young & Weishaar, 1997, p. 76).

As you can see, practice activities of clinical and counseling psychologists are varied. They include, but often not limited to (a) conducting psychotherapy; (b) administering and interpreting psychological tests of personality, intellect, and vocational aptitude; (c) facilitating psychoeducational and psychotherapy groups; and (d) supervising the clinical work of other therapists (Himelein, 1999). Clinical and counseling psychologists work in many different types of settings—and their specific practice activities often vary by setting.

EMPLOYMENT SETTINGS

Private Practice

Students who are interested in clinical and counseling psychology careers often dream of starting a private practice. Twenty percent of counseling psychologists and 40% of clinical psychologists work in private practice settings (Gelso & Fretz, 2001; Trull & Phares, 2001). In private practice, psychologists engage in assessment, diagnosis, and therapy. However, private practice also entails a great deal of administrative work. The changing health care system and movement toward managed care has increased the amount of paperwork. Insurance companies require that psychologists provide extensive documentation to justify treatment sessions (Young & Weishaar, 1997). A great deal of time is also spent billing and collecting, keeping client records and notes, and responding to request for records and treatment summaries. Solo private practice, in which a psychologist works independently—hanging out a shingle, so to speak—is becoming uncommon because insurance companies are providing lower rates of reimbursement than ever before. Most independent practitioners find it difficult to make a living in solo practice. Instead, psychologists are flocking to group practices in which several therapists work together as partners, sharing office space, secretarial help, and other resources (Young & Weishaar, 1997).

College and University Counseling Centers

Many practitioners, particularly counseling psychologists, are employed in college and university counseling centers. Psychologists in these settings help college students deal with developmental issues, such as identity formation, career development, and stress management. They lead focus groups, conduct group therapy, and develop and administer outreach programs to help students with study skills, anger management, communication skills, and more.

Community Mental Health Centers

Clinical and counseling psychologists who seek careers in community mental health centers may work directly with clients, providing therapy and assessment, but more often will engage in administrative roles. Most community mental health centers employ psychologists in administrative positions entailing little direct service. Instead, psychologists in these settings supervise master's level counselors, oversee the center, and engage in program development and evaluation to ensure that the community's needs are met.

Hospitals and Medical Centers

Clinical and counseling psychologists are found in medical settings such as V.A. facilities, hospitals, and even emergency rooms. Psychologists are members of multidisciplinary teams with physicians, nurses, psychiatrists, physicians, mental health counselors, and social workers (Davis, 1997). The multidisciplinary team works together to identify treatment goals, and develop and evaluate treatment plans (Simon & Folen, 2001). In addition to consulting on multidisciplinary teams, psychologists who work in medical settings also develop and implement interventions to address patients' health problems, such as chronic pain, anxiety, hypertension, and more. They also engage in staff development, educating physicians, medical students, and interns about psychological factors that play a role in health and illness (Brown, Freeman, & Brown, 2002), and supervise master's-level clinicians, students, interns, and new psychologists.

ADVANTAGES AND DISADVANTAGES TO A CAREER IN PSYCHOLOGICAL PRACTICE

Advantages to a career in psychological practice include personal fulfillment—helping clients can be very rewarding. As a clinical or counseling psychologist, you can make a difference in someone's life. You're also likely to be confronted with a variety of challenges, that will make your work interesting. Every client is different, so you'll get to work with a variety of problems and issues that can stave off boredom. Clinical and counseling psychologists are continually learning, as our knowledge of psychology and how to apply it in practice is constantly changing. The benefits of psychological practice often vary by setting. For example, psychologists in private practice experience a great deal of autonomy and often express higher levels of job satisfaction than do psychologists in clinics, hospitals, and mental health centers (Glidewell & Livert, 1992).

Disadvantages include long hours. As a practicing psychologist, you often must be available to meet with clients during their free time, which means that evening and weekend work is common. You'll face lots of paperwork, which can be tedious, difficult to organize and take a lot of time. Burnout is possible as therapy is emotionally and psychologically demanding. As with the benefits, disadvantages to a career in psychological practice vary by setting. Psychologists in private practice may experience isolation and financial stress as private practice offers no guaranteed salary or fringe benefits. In medical settings, psychologists often complain of a lack of respect from physicians and express the desire to be treated as an equal colleague (Simon & Folen, 2001). Finally, a career in psychological practice can be financially rewarding, but the rewards are not spread evenly across settings, as is evident by the salaries depicted in Table 2.1.

TABLE 2.1   MEDIAN SALARIES FOR DOCTORAL-LEVEL CAREERS IN DIRECT SERVICE

(Adapted from Singleton, Tate, & Randall, 2003)

	Median Annual Salary ($)
LICENSED CLINICAL PSYCHOLOGISTS (5–9 YEARS' EXPERIENCE)	
University/counseling center	45,000
Public general hospital	57,000
Private general hospital	56,000
Not-for-profit private mental hospital	55,000
V.A. hospital	71,000
Individual private practice	66,000
Group psychological practice	52,000
Medical-psychological group practice	76,500
LICENSED COUNSELING PSYCHOLOGISTS (5–9 YEARS' EXPERIENCE)	
University/college counseling center	47,000
Individual private practice	90,000
Group psychological practice	78,000
Community mental health clinic	62,000

Preparation for a Career in Psychological Practice

If you're interested in engaging in practice as a clinical or counseling psychologist, seek graduate experiences that will enhance your experience as a clinician. Work on developing your therapeutic, listening, and communication skills. Develop a broad base of knowledge and skills because you can't predict the wide range of problems with which you'll be asked to assist clients. Develop proficiency in different types of therapy, seek practice placements in a range of settings, and take advantage of opportunities to attend conferences and workshops that focus on clinical practice (Palmer & Baucom, 1999).

Obtain a solid background in research. Research training is valuable, even for psychologists who plan careers in practice settings. Today's challenging economic environment requires that psychologists demonstrate the efficacy of intervention and treatment (Palmer & Baucom, 1999). The ability to conduct outcomes research is critical to tomorrow's practitioner.

If you're planning on working in a private practice setting, either solo or group practice, take additional courses in financial management and marketing. A private practice is a business and you'll need to become savvy in marketing and promotional techniques to make your small business a success. These business skills aren't taught in clinical and counseling psychology graduate programs, so seek opportunities to develop your business skills through related coursework in other departments. Relatedly, learn about managed care by reading the growing body of literature designed to help psychologists adapt to changing health care delivery systems.

Recommended Readings

American Psychological Association Practice Directorate. (1998). *Practicing psychology in hospitals and other health care facilities.* Washington, DC: Author.

Collison, B. B., & Garfield, N. J. (Eds.). (1996). *Careers in Counseling and Human Services,* (2nd Ed.). New York: Taylor & Francis.

Lopez, S. J., & Prosser, E. C. (2000). Becoming an adaptive new professional: Going beyond Plante's principles. *Professional Psychology: Research & Practice.* 31(4), pp 461–462.

Hayes, S. C., Barlow, D. H., & Nelson-Gray, R. O. (1999). *The scientist practitioner: Research and accountability in the age of managed care* (2nd Ed.). Boston, MA: Allyn & Bacon

Knight, A. (2002). *How to become a clinical psychologist: Getting a foot in the door.* New York: Brunner-Routledge

Martin, I. (1996). *From Couch to Corporation: Becoming a Successful Corporate Therapist.* New York: Wiley.

Means, M. K. (2002). Building a private psychotherapy practice. *Clinical Psychologist, 55*(3) 16–21.

Palmer, C. A., & Baucom, D. H. (1999). Making the most of your clinical PhD: Preparing for a successful career in an evolving and diversified profession. *Clinical Psychologist, 52*(2), 7–17.

Prinstein, M. J., & Patterson, M. D. (2003). *The portable mentor: Expert guide to a successful career in psychology.* New York: Kluwer.

Woody, R. H., & Robertson, M. H. (1997). *A career in clinical psychology: From training to employment.* Madison, CT: International Universities Press.

WEB RESOURCES

A Guide to Psychology and Its Practice
http://www.guidetopsychology.com/be_psy.htm

Careers in Clinical and Counseling Psychology
http://www.wcupa.edu/_ACADEMICS/sch_cas.psy/Career_Paths/Clinical/Career03.htm

Division 12 of the American Psychological Association (Society of Clinical Psychology)
http://www.apa.org/divisions/div12/

Division 17 of the American Psychological Association (Counseling Psychology)
http://www.div17.org/

Graduate Students Contemplating Starting an Independent Practice: Reality or Fantasy
http://www.psychpage.com/ethics/apa_indep_practice.html

Psychology Information Online
http://www.psychologyinfo.com/students/careers-clinical.html

PROFILE 2.1: BRICK JOHNSTONE, PH.D.

Dr. Brick Johnstone is an Associate Professor in the Department of Physical Medicine and Rehabilitation at the University of Missouri Hospital and Clinics. He is the Director of the Division of Clinical Health Psychology and Neuropsychology and is also certified by the American Board of Clinical Neuropsychology. Dr. Johnstone's research focuses on neuropsychological assessment, training in clinical neuropsychology, and health care reform. We asked Dr. Johnstone about his background and his interests, as well as his take on the future of clinical psychology and neuropsychology.

What originally got you interested in the field of clinical psychology?

I became interested in clinical psychology as an undergraduate at Duke University, through both academic coursework and clinical practica. I developed a strong interest in psychopathology based on an abnormal psychology course I took, as well as volunteer activities I engaged in at Butner State Hospital. Coursework in cognitive and perceptual psychology led to my long-term interest in brain functioning and eventually in neuropsychology. Finally, as an undergraduate, I was able to participate as a research assistant on a study determining psychometric correlates of popularity in children, which led to my interest in psychological research.

Describe what activities you are involved in as a clinical psychologist.

I currently serve as the Director of the Division of Clinical Health Psychology and Neuropsychology in the University of Missouri–Columbia Department of Physical Medicine and Rehabilitation. Although I have administrative and research duties, my primary interest is clinical. I am board certified as a neuropsychologist, but view myself as a clinical psychologist who specializes in brain dysfunction. Although I work with a special needs population, the skills I employ are those I was taught in graduate school. My assessment of patients is based primarily on a detailed clinical interview and behavioral observations, and secondly on objective test data. My treatment of patients with brain dysfunction is based on all the behavioral treatment methods I learned in my clinical psychology graduate program at the University of Georgia.

Consistent with trends suggesting that clinical psychologists will need to develop administrative skills in the future, I am also the administrator for a division of seven psychologists, six postdoctoral fellows, two interns, and numerous staff members. Unfortunately my graduate training did not prepare me for many of the financial and political issues we face today, and it is my hope that our graduate programs can do a better job of educating our future students in these areas. My research focus has been on demonstrating the functional utility of neuropsychological evaluations. I am currently the primary investigator (PI) for one of 17 national Traumatic Brain Injury Model Systems Centers, and it is important to note that 12 of the 17 PIs for these grants are psychologists. Opportunities for clinical psychologists to expand in numerous areas of health care and health policy are extraordinary.

What are your particular areas of expertise or interest?

My main area of expertise is neuropsychology. In graduate school, I completed a summer externship at the Kansas City V.A. Hospital in neuropsychology, even though I had never even administered a WAIS before that. That experience solidified my interest in working with individuals with brain dysfunction. My clinical and research interests involve making neuropsychological evaluations more functionally relevant. As a result of historical factors, the specialty of neuropsychology evolved primarily to assist with diagnosing various disorders and identify brain-behavior relationships. However, with the advent of sophisticated neuroradiological techniques, neuropsychology needs to become more functionally relevant and focus on practical treatment strategies for individuals with brain injury and their families. I have learned much regarding rehabilitation psychology from my colleagues in the Department of Physical Medicine and Rehabilitation, and it is my goal to improve neuropsychological treatments for individuals with brain dysfunction and update training guidelines for neuropsychologists to include better training in rehabilitation and disability issues.

What are the future trends you see in clinical psychology?

It is always entertaining to project the future of psychology, particularly given the potential growth opportunities as well as stressors related to managed care. On the positive side, clinical psychologists continue to expand their expertise into areas outside of traditional mental health. At my current setting, clinical psychologists are primarily investigators on Robert Wood Johnson Foundation grants focusing on (1) developing Medicaid managed care programs for individuals with disabilities and (2) investigating the impact of managed care on children with disabilities in rural settings. Other psychologists in our division are primarily investigators on grants investigating the use of telemedicine applications for individuals with traumatic brain injury in rural settings, and one colleague is the only psychologist who is a PI for one of the 17 national Spinal Cord Injury Model Systems. In addition, many medical school psychologists are identifying numerous medical populations that can benefit from psychological services (including those with systemic illnesses, infectious diseases, and cardiovascular diseases).

Managed care trends have had positive effects in that they have forced all health care professionals to better demonstrate the effectiveness of our services. However, because we have not demonstrated that psychologists can provide superior and less expensive services than social workers and licensed professional counselors, there is a good chance that clinical positions for psychologists will decrease in the future. As president of the Missouri Psychological Association, I have learned that the future of clinical psychology rests on our shoulders, including our ability to advocate for our profession and demonstrate our value to others. If we do not do it for ourselves, no one else will.

What are some future trends you see in neuropsychology?

I see the specialty of neuropsychology diverging in two directions. The first will be toward an experimental focus, with more research identifying specific brain-behavior relationships. Sophisticated neuroradiological techniques will allow us to gain a much better understanding of how the brain works. On the other hand, I foresee clinical neuropsychology focusing on the development of rehabilitation-based assessment and treatment. In the future, most individuals who are referred for neuropsychology evaluations will have known etiologies for their difficulties. Therefore, clinical neuropsychologists will need to develop specific treatment recommendations to assist individuals in their daily functions, at home, work, or school.

(Reprinted with permission of Trull & Phares, 2001.)

PROFILE 2.2: STUART TENTONI, PH.D.

Dr. Stuart Tentoni is Senior Psychologist and Coordinator/Training Director for the University of Wisconsin–Milwaukee Norris Student Health Center. He earned his Ph.D. from North Texas State University in 1974 at age 24, and was the youngest doctoral graduate in the history of the department. Over the years he has practiced in a variety of areas, including geropsychology, alcohol and drug rehabilitation, and developmental disabilities. Dr. Tentoni has held teaching positions in both the clinical psychology and educational psychology programs at UWM from 1991 to 1998. In 2002, Dr. Tenoni received the Raymond D. Fowler Award, given annually by the American Psychological Association of Graduate Students to a psychologist who has made an outstanding contribution to the professional development of students. I asked Dr. Tentoni about his background and experience, as well as his take on developing a career in psychology.

How did you become interested in psychology?

I started my undergraduate studies back in 1966 at the Wisconsin State University–Oshkosh, and vacillated between being a pre-med major or a pre-dental major. At the end of my sophomore year, I found out that I would be required to take "gross anatomy" as a medical student. That meant spending a year dissecting a cadaver. I lost all interest in a medical career after that. As much as I hate to admit this, I checked the university catalog to see what I could major in that required the fewest number of credits and that I already had most of the prerequisite courses for, and that field was psychology. Having 57 credits of math and science as an undergraduate, I was poorly prepared for the amount of reading that psychology was going to require and did not do well in the major until the last semester of my senior year.

I took my first "counseling" course, and the course instructor was a practicing psychologist at the Winnebago Mental Health Institute. We had to write a class paper on the Freudians and Neo-Freudians and I wrote on Harry Stack Sullivan. It was the first "A" paper I had ever written and the instructor made a notation on my paper that he wanted to meet me after the class. I was sort of a "hippy" back then with long hair and beard, and the instructor wasn't expecting a person looking like me to be the one who had written the paper I did, but he got over it quickly and asked me if I had ever considered going into counseling as a field of endeavor. I hadn't, but strongly considered it given how well I did in the counseling course. The only glitch I ran into was the psychology department emphasis was "general/experimental" and they did not have a clinical psychology or counseling psychology program.

The option left to me was to apply for graduate admission into the School of Education's program in Counselor Education. I started that program in Fall 1970 and completed my master's degree in December 1971. Deciding to make a clean sweep of graduate school, I applied to and enrolled into the Counselor Education program in the School of Education at North Texas State University in Denton, Texas (now the University of North Texas) in January 1972 and finished my Ph.D. in May 1974, becoming the youngest graduate in the history of my program. I was a month short of turning 25 years of age. The instructor who made all of this possible, by merely putting the thought into my head was Robert G. Lane, who left the profession to become a novelist in the early 1980's. He authored the novel, *A Solitary Dance*.

What are your particular areas of expertise or interest?

Those who preceded me in the profession told me to make sure I had a little experience and proficiency in virtually everything. I took that recommendation literally. Although my doctorate is in "counselor education," I am neither a "counselor" nor an "educator." I was required to minor in clinical psychology and I took courses in individual appraisal (intelligence testing); personality testing (Minnesota Multiphasic Personality Inventory); and projective testing (Rorschach technique, using the Beck scoring system). The licensing laws for psychologists back in the 1970's indicated that equal consideration would be given to doctoral graduates from clinical psychology, counseling psychology, guidance, counseling, and educational psychology programs. Those laws have long since changed, as those with counseling degrees can obtain licensure as "professional counselors" in many states.

I have been in clinical practice since May 1974, working over 2 years as a consulting psychologist with geriatric and developmentally disabled populations. I spent 15 months doing testing and interpretive sessions in an inpatient alcohol and drug treatment facility. From that, I worked a day over 11 years in a county-operated mental health center and outpatient clinic as the first psychologist to have formal training and work experience working in all three areas of disability (mental health, alcohol/drug, and developmentally disabled). Halfway through that stint, I did over 90% of the forensic assessments done by the county outpatient clinic and also those that came to me by a request from the court itself.

In 1989, I decided that I wanted to spend a portion of my remaining career working in the setting I was formally trained to work in, that being a university counseling center. The University of Wisconsin–Milwaukee hired me to work in the student health center, which contained both medical and psychological services for our campus of 30,000 students. I no longer do psychological testing, and the clients I specialize with are those with chronic mental health problems, chronic health problems, couples therapy (both gay and straight), alcohol and drug problems, and students with criminal backgrounds.

Describe your employment setting and the activities in which you engage? How do you spend your days?

My current setting is the Norris Health Center on the University of Wisconsin–Milwaukee campus. The campus counseling center is located in the Health Center, where we are physically, fiscally, and administratively housed. We have slightly under five full-time staff to handle the emotional issues and concerns of 30,000 students. Students pay a segregated fee as part of their overall tuition bill and the Health Center services are a part of that fee. Student fees fund approximately 95% of what goes on in our building, so we have developed a strong sense of obligation toward the students who fund the service.

My responsibilities are to do initial assessments with students seeking counseling service to determine if we can help them at all (problems that are of a long term duration might result in our having to refer a student to a mental health provider in the community), and whether I might be the provider they should be seeing to resolve their issue(s). In addition to that, I am the coordinator for the counseling department, meaning that I field a number of calls from those wanting to know more about what services we offer; I handle calls from the media on local issues that might crop up; and I handle all the complaints.

My coordinator duties also have me directing the day-to-day operations of the counseling unit, as well as providing clinical supervision to the counseling staff and the seven consulting psychiatry residents we had with us during the past academic year. I also have to compile data on service utilization by students so that staff can focus on treating students and I will take care of the accountability to those over me in the management hierarchy. I am to spend approximately 80% of my work week doing intake assessments and individual treatment with students in need of our services. The remaining time is spent in my administrative duties, which often is not enough time to get those duties done. During the academic year, it is not uncommon for me to be scheduled to see seven students per day, with 1 hour for writing up intake assessments and progress notes. I come in to work up to 30 minutes early and leave up to an hour late just to get everything else done.

What are the advantages and disadvantages of your career choice and setting?

There are a number of advantages of working in my particular setting. Generally, college or university counseling jobs are highly prized and competition for them can become rather fierce. Seventy-two psychologists applied in 1989 for one of the two vacant positions at the University of Wisconsin–Milwaukee, and I was lucky enough to be one of the two selected for the post. The salary offered for what I do is pretty good, although I have 30 years of post-doctoral experience and know of many others in settings similar to mine who make more than I do (my salary is a matter of public record and is $73,208 as of July 1, 2004). I receive a liberal amount of vacation time and holidays off, with the biggest advantage I receive being that of funding and time for continuing education and professional activities. My institution provides me with $1,500 a year and 7 work days to get the continuing education I need to maintain my license as a psychologist in the State of Wisconsin. This would be difficult for me to do on my own if the responsibility was all mine to do. I am given time to provide clinical supervision to doctoral psychology students desiring practicum placements to learn more about psychotherapy, and I am encouraged to do research and write if I want.

The university environment seldom gets boring and continues to be a vibrant setting to work in. Students are generally bright and motivated and want help, with many of them succeeding at resolving their concerns and then recommending their friends to us. I work closely with the four other counseling staff members, and because we are such a small counseling department, our jobs do have a measure of security that counselors in other settings wish they had.

Disadvantages of my particular setting involve money, as the amount of raise we are allowed is controlled by the Wisconsin legislators. It is very difficult to get to the top of one's salary range, if it even happens. Opportunities for ad-

vancement are limited, as most universities operate under the "faculty gover-
nance" system, which typically mandates that to be considered for high-level
administrative positions, one must be a tenured faculty member. I work for the
"Student Affairs" division, which will be headed up by a tenured faculty member in the very near future.

The biggest disadvantage has occurred for me as I have gotten older, and
that is that because of my age, students are viewing me as though I am their
"older parent," or even as a "grandparent." Our culture does not typically hold
those older in much esteem, and that has played itself out with a number of
students I have seen in the past couple years. I would estimate I have less than
2 years left in this setting because of my age.

Another disadvantage that has occurred periodically has occurred when
our health center had medical doctors as directors of the combined facility.
There are many times that the "medical model" and the "psychological services
model" have clashed and our medical director either asked or mandated that
we do things a certain way that might be unethical. We managed to resolve
one instance informally, and I had to call in both the State of Wisconsin Psychology Examining Board and the American Psychological Association in once
to resolve the other.

In considering a career like mine, prospective students would be well
served by realizing they will never get "rich" by doing this kind of work. To be
successful at it, one must really, really, REALLY like people and want to help
them. And, those you help will be able to determine very quickly if you are fak-
ing it or not.

How can students prepare themselves for a career in psychological practice?

To prepare for a career such as mine, I would strongly recommend that you be
a better student than I was. I still am not sure if I picked psychology (in the form
of "counselor education") or if it picked me. I was not prepared for the length
and intensity of the reading assignments I had as an undergraduate. You must
know as early as possible if you want to be a psychologist or not because no
matter how you cut it, you are looking at a minimum of 8 years of academic
study to obtain the doctoral degree. It takes a great amount of academic am-
bition to go all the way for a doctoral degree.

My suggestion is to be aware of the general formula used by psychology departments to determine who they will admit to graduate study. The general formula
consists of (1) your undergraduate GPA; (2) your GPA during your last 2 years of
undergraduate study; (3) your GPA in your major; (4) your GRE scores (verbal and
math); and (5) recommendations from professors you took psychology courses

from or may have helped do research. At the same time, the best piece of advice I was given about school is that if I was going to continue on for graduate level work, I should go straight through and get all the degrees there were, without taking any time off for jobs, etc. The reason is that if one takes time off, it becomes hard to go back to reading texts and taking tests.

I am near the age end-point of the "baby boomer" generation, or those who were born after World War II. We are not going to work as long as our parents did. Many of us will be retiring in the next 5 years or so and there needs to be someone to replace us once we leave the work force. The population is increasing, as are the problems that population has. They aren't going to get help from *Dr. Phil* or the myriad of talk shows on television. Hopefully, they will get it from you.

PROFILE 2.3: MARILU PRICE BERRY, PH.D.

Dr. Marilu Price Berry is an Assistant Professor in the Department of Anesthesiology at the University of Texas at Houston (UT–H) Health Science Center. Since completing a postdoctoral fellowship in behavioral medicine and pain management in 1999, she has been a staff psychologist at the UT–H affiliated University Center for Pain Medicine and Rehabilitation at Memorial Hermann. Lu completed a Ph.D. in Counseling Psychology at Texas A&M University and a pre-doctoral internship at the Puget Sound Health Care System, Seattle VA Division. As faculty for the UT–H Medical School, she is involved in training medical students, residents, and fellows in anesthesiology as they rotate through the Pain Center. While actively involved in the pain community of the Texas Medical Center in Houston, she provides lectures on interdisciplinary treatment of chronic pain in the community and managed care organizations.

Her research interests include psychological screening for implantable devices, interdisciplinary treatment of chronic pain, somatization, utilization of pain as the fifth vital sign, anxiety and breast biopsy, and post-traumatic stress disorder and pain. In her clinical work she provides behavioral medicine services such as biofeedback and relaxation training, psychoeducational lectures, and individual, couple, and group psychotherapy. I asked Dr. Berry about her background and experience, as well as her recommendations on developing a career in health psychology, a popular practice specialty.

Describe your background. How did you become interested in psychology?

I grew up with a psychiatrist as a mother, and the way she talked about her work made it sound so interesting. She had a private practice of therapy patients with various problems (depression, anxiety, schizophrenia, marital problems) and seemed to love her work.

In college I took some psychology classes and found it intriguing hearing about why people did some of the kooky things they did. Abnormal psychology and personality theories were two of my favorite courses. Then I did a research project interviewing veterans at a nearby hospital, and I was hooked.

What are your particular areas of expertise or interest?

Initially I focused my studies and clinical work on trauma. I have worked with combat veterans, victims of abuse, and sexual assault survivors. Along the way I did clinical practica in medical settings and learned how exciting and challenging that was. My current area of expertise is health psychology, more specifically working with people who have chronic pain and medical problems that are long term. I also still see people who have been traumatized, but now the trauma is more likely to be a severe injury with amputation.

Describe your employment setting. How do you spend your days?

I work in an outpatient pain clinic housed inside a large hospital. People who have pain that won't go away are referred to us to help them cope with the pain. I work on a team with physicians, and we use a combined approach of medications, injections, exercise, and psychotherapy to help them. I see patients in individual therapy and teach them techniques for coping with the pain and stress of having pain. Sometimes I train them in relaxation and biofeedback techniques to lower their muscle tension; other times I teach them to distract themselves or do things differently to avoid reinjury. Many times I see the patient with their spouse or partner to talk about how the pain is affecting their relationship and to teach the significant other how to help the patient. Sometimes I see patients in their hospital rooms after they have had surgery or when they are facing bad news like a cancer diagnosis.

Since I am on faculty at the medical school, part of my job is to train medical students, residents, and fellows. I teach them how to talk to patients about difficult things like sex, homosexuality, and substance abuse. I teach them how to recognize depression and anxiety in medical patients and how to phrase the referral to a mental health treatment provider.

What are the advantages and disadvantages of your career choice and setting? What should students know in considering such a career?

Health psychology is a great career. I enjoy learning about medical problems, anatomy, and medications, and I am never bored. It is interesting and exciting to work in a medical setting and be around life-or-death issues. I work with a relatively "normal" population of people who have medical problems but who may have been fully functioning and not depressed or anxious before their injury or diagnosis.

The disadvantages are related to the medical setting. Sometimes psychologists are seen as "second class citizens" by physicians and are not valued as highly in the medical hierarchy. Also, I have worked with people who ended up dying or very disfigured from their injury or illness, and this is upsetting if you are not well prepared for it.

This career requires flexibility, interest in learning new things, and comfort in a medical setting. A health psychologist must have good verbal and written communication skills and be able to use them with referring physicians and patients.

How can students prepare themselves for such a career?

The best way to prepare yourself for a career as a health psychologist is to get training and experience. After college you should attend graduate school to get a Ph.D. or Psy.D. in psychology, and this may take 5–7 more years of school. Along the way you can find opportunities to be in a medical setting and see if you like it. This can be done in clinical practica, internships, research projects, or volunteer work. You can take classes in health psychology, and some graduate programs have a specialty track or even a whole program in this area. This journey takes a long time and lots of school, but at the end the career is worth it and you'll have lots of interesting stories to tell.

PROFILE 2.4: BRIAN R. SNIDER, PH.D.

Brian R. Snider, Ph.D., is a licensed Health Service Psychologist in Oklahoma. He earned his doctoral degree in applied behavioral studies at Oklahoma State University with a specialty in counseling psychology. His areas of professional interest include anxiety disorders, psychological assessment, and parent training.

Describe your backround. How did you become interested in psycholgy?

I was originally involved in the "hard sciences" as an undergraduate. I have always leaned toward the helping professions, but became more interested in psychology after taking undergraduate psychology courses. I really liked the "culture" of the psychology department which seemed more relaxed and supportive than the stories I had heard about medical school, etc. Another influence for me was my grandmother, who was a paraprofessional counselor for her church. Many of my memories of her center around her kindness in helping others.

What are you particular areas of expertise or interest?

I consider myself a general practitioner who treats nearly anyone who walks into my office. It is interesting how practice niches develop, sometime unwittingly. I just happened to receive a couple of referrals from insurance companies for pre-surgical evaluations for gastric bypass candidates. These patients told me their difficulties in finding a provider for these evaluations. I did some low-level marketing to several surgeons and now have a steady stream of referrals from them.

I am also currently in the process of developing a niche practice with a colleague that focuses on anxiety disorders. We will concentrate our marketing on primary care physicians, who often are the gatekeepers for referrals to specialized mental health care.

I also tend to perform a lot of psychological evaluations. Many are attention deficit-hyperactivity disorder evaluations with both children and adults. Additionally, I do many state-contracted mental status evaluations for people pplying for Social Security disability benefits. Oftentimes, these assessments will involve administering Minnesota Multiphasic Personality Inventory-2 intelligence tests.

Describe your employment setting and the activities in which you engage. How do you spend your days?

I work in a private practice setting with two licensed professional counselors. We also have an office manager who performs support staff duties. I typically see six patients per day for individual therapy, couples/marital/family therapy, or psychological evaluations. When I am not seeing patients, I write progress notes, return phone calls, write psych reports, request treatment authorizations, tend to business or financial issues, and market my practice.

What are the advantages and disadvantages of your career choice and setting? What should students know in considering such a career?

The principal advantage of private practice psychology is autonomy and "being my own boss". I can tailor my practice any way that I please. My schedule is flexible, and I can see patients whenever I want. The iterations of ways in which private practice is autonomous is nearly endless. Private practice can be lucrative if you are good at your craft and have a basic grasp of marketing.

Although I share office space with two other clinicians, we all eat what we kill, so to speak. If you are not a good hunter, you can starve in private practice. If I don't see patients due to low referrals, illness, vacation, etc., I don't get paid. This fragile nature of income is the primary drawback of private practice. Generally, I enjoy the business aspect of private practice; however, the accounting aspect can be very cumbersome.

A student should consider if a career in private practice suits his or her personality. If one is generally anxiety-ridden about finances and values monetar security above all else, private practice (or self-employment in general, is likely not a good career choice. Additionally, a person who is bored stiff with business matters should probably steer clear of private practice. Conversely, if one is a dreamer, enjoys a certain amount of risk, and likes (or at least tolerates) business, private practice can be invigorating.

How can students prepare themselves for such a career?

An obvious cornerstone of successful private practice is sound clinical skills. Another foundational element that must be in place for private practice is some knowledge of business. A lack of business savvy is likely a major reason for private practice failures. Students can prepare themselves with some basic education business accounting, marketing, and small-business ownership. Frequently, mini-course that cover these topics are offered at community colleges or technical/vocational schools. Many books are dedicated to this subject as well. The bottom line is that a private practice is a business and should be run like one.

CAREERS IN PUBLIC HEALTH AND POLICY

CHAPTER GUIDE

WHAT IS PUBLIC HEALTH?

EMPLOYMENT SETTINGS

CAREER TRACKS
RESEARCH
POLITICS
PROGRAM DEVELOPMENT AND
EVALUATION

PREPARATION FOR A CAREER IN
PUBLIC HEALTH AND SOCIAL
POLICY

RECOMMENDED READINGS

WEB RESOURCES

PROFILE 3.1: SIMON H.
BUDMAN, PH.D.

PROFILE 3.2: MONICA BASKIN,
PH.D.

PROFILE 3.3: APA'S
CONGRESSIONAL AND
EXECUTIVE BRANCH
FELLOWSHIP PROGRAM

Psychological research holds implications for public health and social policy, decisions about issues that affect the quality of human life, such as health care, education, welfare, crime and violence prevention, and other social issues (Levant et al., 2001). Psychologists can inform and contribute to policy development in many ways. Psychologists' skills in identifying and conceptualizing health and social problems are valuable in determining when policy is needed (Fowler, 1996). Planning solutions to problems, policy formation, is aided by psychologists' abilities to synthesize the relevant scientific literature, design and carry out pilot studies, and evaluate potential solutions. Implementing solutions to public health and social problems, such as carrying out intervention and prevention programs, relies on psychologists' interpersonal, therapeutic, and administrative skills. Finally, psychologists' research skills come to bear in evaluating and improving the effectiveness of public health and social policy solutions (Fowler, 1996). Clearly, psychologists can provide critical contributions to policy formation and evaluation. In this chapter, you'll learn about several ways in which clinical and counseling psychologists can become social activists and get involved in public health and social policy.

WHAT IS PUBLIC HEALTH?

Public health is "the science and art of preventing disease, prolonging life, and promoting health and efficiency through organized community effort" (Institute of Medicine, 1988). It's an interdisciplinary field that addresses the physical, psychological, and environmental health concerns of communities and groups at risk for illness and injury by applying health promotion and disease prevention technologies and interventions designed to improve and enhance quality of life. Specifically, the mission of public health includes the following (Association of Schools of Public Health, 1994):

• Assess and monitor the community to identify health problems, hazards, and priorities
•Work with community and government leaders to formulate public policies to address local and national health problems and priorities
•Educate and empower people about health issues
•Improve access to appropriate and cost-effective health care and evaluating the effectiveness of health care
•Research new solutions to health problems

Clinical and counseling psychologists' research on health, disease, wellness, and risk behavior is critical to achieving the mission of public health.

EMPLOYMENT SETTINGS

Psychologists with interests in public health and policy are found in many settings, including academia, government, and practice, setting. They are employed as professors in departments of psychology and schools of public health and social policy, where they teach and conduct research (as described in Chapter 7). They also work in local and state departments of public health where they hold leadership positions such as director of health education programs, coordinator of local prevention efforts (e.g., drug-alcohol prevention), manager of community relations, and consultant or advisor on local or state initiatives (e.g., commission on women's/men's/minority health). Nonprofit (e.g., American Cancer Society) and for-profit (e.g., Research Triangle Institute) agencies and the federal government (e.g., Centers for Disease Control and Prevention) employ psychologists as project managers and directors to oversee various projects and funded grants (Baskin, in press).

CAREER TRACKS

There are several career tracks for psychologists with interests in public health and social policy. Specific professional activities and responsibilities entailed vary with the position and employment setting.

Research

Psychologists influence social policy by conducting research that sheds light on important health and social problems (e.g., influence of health care accessibility on health status, predictors of violence, and the impact of welfare reform on the welfare of low-income families). Psychologists who conduct policy-related research may work within traditional academic settings (i.e., colleges and universities), government positions (e.g., National Institutes of Mental Health, National Institute on Drug Abuse), and at think tanks or policy-oriented organizations that resemble academia (Kuther & Morgan, 2004). They might lobby and inform legislators about their research findings as well as other relevant findings from the psychology literature. Other psychologists (regardless of work setting, academic or otherwise) might provide expert testimony during congressional hearings to educate legislators about psychological issues that bear on public policy (Wrightsman, 2001). Psychologists may be asked to participate in committees to draft *amicus curiae* briefs on behalf of the American Psychological Association (a professional organization for psychologists). An amicus curiae brief is "a stylized instrument for combining facts, law, and logic as needed to present judges with the most compelling argument for adopting whatever position the filer advocates" (Tremper, 1987, p. 496). In other words, it's a formal way of educating legislators about research findings pertinent to a particular policy issue.

Research psychologists within academia may engage in any of these activities as an extension of their policy-related research. As we will discuss in Chapter 7, academic careers offer a flexible schedule, autonomy, and prestige. Disadvantages of a research career in academia include competition (i.e., academic positions are scarce), long hours, and pressure to publish. Many psychologists engage in policy-related research careers outside of academia, in nonprofit agencies and think tanks.

Psychologists employed at nonprofit agencies and think tanks conduct research to assess and improve the effectiveness of intervention and prevention programs, examine social problems and potential solutions, and lobby legislative bodies. The government often contracts nonprofit agencies and think tanks to conduct policy analyses, literature reviews, and research to improve decision-making by political leaders and consumers. If you choose a career in policy at a nonprofit or think tank, much of your time will be spent writing grants, conducting research, analyzing the impact of various policies, and writing, presenting, and publishing your work in various formats to ensure that your findings are accessible to the public and to policy makers. For examples of think tanks and policy-related organizations, see Table 3.1.

TABLE 3.1   THINK TANKS AND POLICY-RELATED ORGANIZATIONS

American Enterprise Institute
    http://www.aei.org/

The Brookings Institution
    http://www.brook.edu/

Center for Health Care Strategies
    http://www.chcs.org/

Center for Studying Health System Change
    http://www.hschange.com/

Children's Defense Fund
    http://www.childrensdefense.org/

Families and Work Institute
    http://www.familiesandwork.org

Manpower Demonstration Research Corporation
    http://www.mdrc.org

The National Center for Policy Analysis
    http://www.ncpa.org/

RAND
    http://www.rand.org

The primary benefit of conducting policy-related research is that your work may lead to social change and can improve the health of individuals in communities. Public health and social policy research are interdisciplinary, which means that if you choose a policy-related career, you'll work with a diverse range of specialists in other fields. Researchers in think tanks and policy-oriented organizations earn salaries similar to those in academia (see Chapter 7). In 1999, for example, doctoral degree holders with 2 to 4 years of experience earned a median salary of $55,000 in nonprofit research settings (Williams, Wicherski, & Kohout, 2000).

Politics

Psychologists are valued on Capitol Hill. Some psychologists get involved in influencing social policy by assisting members of Congress as congressional fellows or as staff members. The American Psychological Association Congressional Fellow program provides psychologists with policy experience and prepares them for policy careers. Goals of the APA Congressional Fellowship program are: "(a) to enable scientists to share their knowledge with legislators so that these lawmakers might be better able to make policies based on professional expertise, and (b) to allow scientists to share with colleagues in their field an 'insider's' understanding of the policy-making process and their potential role in it" (Vincent, 1990, p. 61).

Fellows serve a 1 or 2 year assignment to a staff position in Congress. Fellows perform as regular staff members and are involved in legislative, investigative, and oversight activities. They may develop briefs, conduct policy and psycholegal research, and become involved in planning strategies and drafting laws (American Psychological Association, 2002). Congressional fellows participate in face-to-face briefings with members of Congress, assist in providing information for legislation debated on the floor of the House or Senate, and represent congresspeople at meetings with lobbyists and constituents (Fowler, 1996). About half of fellows later take policy-related positions with federal agencies, Congress, or policy research organizations (Fowler, 1996).

Advantages of a congressional fellowship or staff member position include firsthand participation in policy formation, promoting social change, and making a difference. Psychologists who choose this career path must become generalists in the sense that they will deal with volumes of information on a wide array of subjects. A policy career is fast paced and toilsome, but rewarding. Entry-level psychologist fellows in the American Psychological Association Fellowship program earn approximately $48,500 with a range increasing to $63,100, depending on level of experience. For information about other Congressional fellowship programs, see Table 3.2.

TABLE 3.2   PUBLIC POLICY FELLOWSHIP PROGRAMS

American Association for the Advancement of Science: Policy Fellowships
    http://fellowships.aaas.org/

APA Congressional Fellowship Program
    http://www.apa.org/ppo/funding/congfell.html

Catherine Acuff Congressional Fellowship
    http://www.apa.org/ppo/funding/cathfell.html

Society for Research in Child Development: Congressional and Executive Branch Fellowships
    http://www.srcd.org/policyfellowships.html

White House Fellows Program
    http://www.whitehouse.gov/fellows/

William A. Bailey AIDS Policy Congressional Fellowship
    http://www.apa.org/ppo/funding/baileyfell.html

Program Development and Evaluation

Psychologists with interests in promoting public health often obtain careers in program development and evaluation—a form of applied research. They develop and test the efficacy of interventions in clinic and real-life settings. For example, psychologists might develop and test the following prevention and intervention programs (Bruzzese, in press):

•an educational program to teach high school students with asthma self-regulatory skills to effectively manage their disease
•a school-based intervention to treat social anxiety disorders in adolescents
•an intervention to improve parenting skills in caregivers of 11- to 14-year-olds in order to prevent substance use in the adolescents
•programs to strengthen families of preschoolers from socio-economically disadvantaged communities through parent-to-parent networks in order to promote child social and academic competence and preventing mental health problems, school failure, and juvenile delinquency
•intervention programs applied immediately following trauma to prevent posttraumatic stress disorder
•programs to prevent adolescent pregnancy and improve parenting skills of adolescent parents

Psychologists take leadership roles in designing, implementing, and evaluating prevention and intervention programs. Such work entails a myriad of tasks, such as supervising staff in recruiting and enrolling participants, program implementation, and data entry (Bruzzese, in press). Because program development and evaluation is applied research, a great deal of time is devoted to data analysis, including working closely with database analysts to create comprehensive databases that are easy to use. As data are analyzed, the results are disseminated at professional meetings and in publications. The results are then used to modify and improve the program. Most psychologists who work in program development and evaluation monitor several interventions and gradually develop new programs too.

In addition to research-related activities, careers in program development and evaluation also entail administrative duties, such as the human resource issues of hiring staff and scheduling vacation time, monitoring budgets to ensure money is spent as proposed, and writing yearly reports to the funding agents summarizing the past year's progress and future plans (Bruzzese, in press). Lots of time is spent searching for and applying to sources of funding, which can be stressful. The uncertainty of funding is a potential disadvantage to a career in program development and evaluation. However, an important benefit of this career is making a difference—your work improves people's lives.

PREPARATION FOR A CAREER IN PUBLIC HEALTH AND SOCIAL POLICY

The research basis of public health and social policy work is apparent throughout this chapter. If you're interested in a career in public health and social policy, seek opportunities to obtain research experience. More importantly, look for opportunities to engage in applied research because you must learn how to formulate research questions in ways that can inform policy (Susman-Stillman et al., 1996). Take communications courses to learn how to communicate research findings with a wide and varied audience. Keep up to date on policy issues by reading daily newspapers and policy-related Websites (see the Web Resources at the end of this chapter). Finally, seek a policy-related fellowship and get hands-on learning to supplement your graduate training.

RECOMMENDED READINGS

Pickett, G. E., Pickett, T. W., & Sacks, T. J. (1995). *Opportunities in public health careers.* Lincolnwood, IL: NTC Contemporary.

Schneiderman, N., Speers, M. A., Silva, J. M., Tomes, H., & Gentry, J. H. (Eds.). (2001). *Integrating behavioral social sciences with public health.* Washington, DC: American Psychological Association.

Stoto, M. A., Abel, C. H., & Dievler, A. (1996). *Healthy communities: New partnerships for the future of public health.* Washington, DC: National Academy Press.

Sussman, S. (Ed.). (2000). *Handbook of program development for health behavior research and Practice.* Thousand Oaks, CA:Sage.

WEB RESOURCES

American Public Health Assocaition
  http://www.apha.org/

A Successful Marriage of Psychology and Public Health
  http://www.apa.org/monitor/mar01/publichealth.html

Association of Schools of Public Helath
  http://www.asph.org

Careers in Public Health
  http://www.hsph.harvard.edu/careers/guide-careers.html

Public Health Degree Planner
  http://commprojects.jhsph.edu/degreematrix/CareersAll.cfm

PROFILE 3.1: SIMON H. BUDMAN, PH.D.

Dr. Simon H. Budman is the founder and president of Innovative Training Systems, a private company that provides consultation, training, and products to health care providers and institutions. Dr. Budman has held numerous academic and hospital appointments as well, and he has been intimately involved in implementing managed behavioral health care at several institutions. Dr. Budman is well known for his work in the areas of time-effective (time-limited) treatment, group psychotherapy, and psychotherapy research. He has authored more than 100 books, chapters, articles, as well as several videotapes used in training health care professionals. Dr. Budman has received more than 25 federal grants to support his research in substance abuse, eating disorders, smoking cessation, and many other areas. We asked Dr. Budman several questions about his predictions for the field of clinical psychology and for group psychotherapy.

What originally interested you in the field of clinical psychology?

I had planned to be a physician from the time I was in elementary school. This was mostly based on my experiences with the two local doctors in the town in which I grew up. This was during the 1950s, when doctors still made house calls and had no high-tech tools and little more than penicillin at their disposal. Also, there was no managed care, nor productivity pressures on most of them. An important part of a doctor's intervention at that time was talking to people! I naively believed that this was what being a doctor was about. Entering college in the 1960s as a premed student, I was quickly disillusioned to find that my courses had more to do with biology and chemistry than with people and their behaviors. I quickly quit premed as a major and wandered through a half-dozen other possibilities before a college career counselor told me about clinical psychology and introduced me to a psychologist at the counseling center. My love for psychology was immediate. It had all of the components and more that I thought would exist in medicine, but didn't. I have never had a day of regret since that time about my career choice.

Describe what activities you are involved in as a clinical psychologist.

I started out doing mostly direct clinical work in individual, group, and family therapy (all of which I still do). Over the years, however, my activities changed and diversified. I began to do clinical research shortly after graduate school and have done, and continue to do, numerous clinical trials. I also do extensive training, clinical consulting, and organizational consulting. At present, I am the president of a company that does consulting and training and develops new health care products. In this role, I do a lot of administration, research, marketing, business development, and training. A large part of my time is now spent developing multimedia health care programs and health-related Web sites, writing grants, raising money for the company, and working with teams of psychologists, programmers, businesspeople, and so on. I would never have imagined, even 10 years ago, the types of things I would be doing that are related (both directly and indirectly) to my psychology training.

What are your particular areas of expertise of interest?

At present, I am most interested in population-based health interventions, preventive behavioral health care, behavioral oncology, substance abuse treatment and prevention, and the use of computers, the Internet, and multimedia technology in health care. I have written or cowritten video programs and multimedia games for teens.

What are the future trends you see for clinical psychology?

I think that the future is grave unless clinical psychology is flexible and can "reinvent" itself. Social workers, nurses, and master's-level counselors will do more of the outpatient and inpatient therapy that goes on in this country. Jobs for clinical psychologists will become scarcer than they are already. Incomes will go down. I foresee a grim future, unless psychologists learn unique skills such as how to intervene with populations of people and how to use new technologies in support of such interventions. Although I believe that there will always be a need for clinical psychologists to provide direct clinical care, there is currently a glut of providers in this country who can offer such services. Clinical psychology will look very different ten years from now than it does today. If it doesn't reinvent itself, it will blend in with and be indistinct from the other behavioral health professions.

(Reprinted with permission from Trull & Phares, 2001)

Profile 3.2: Monica L. Baskin, Ph.D.

Monica L. Baskin, Ph.D., is an Assistant Professor in the Department of Health Behavior at the University of Alabama at Birmingham School of Public Health and Associate Science in the UAB Clinical Nutrition Center (NIH-funded), UAB Center for Health Promotion (CDC-funded), and the UAB Minority Health and Research Center. She received a B.A. in psychology and sociology from Emory University, and an M.S. in Community couseling and a Ph.D. in counseling psychology from Georgia State University.

Describe your background. How did you become interested in psychology?

I am a licensed psychologist with extensive training in child/pediatric psychology.

I first became interested in psychology because of my father's interest in the same. He majored in psychology and minored in physical education and religion in college. He often spoke about the connection between mind, body, and spirit and his interest in learning more about how these three things influence human behavior. I shared his intrigue as a young person and further discovered a desire to assist minority persons, such as myself, to deal with the stressors of day-to-day difficulties.

I particularly have chosen to work with children and adolescence as it is my belief that this is a critical time for growth and correction, which are often more difficult to achieve later in life.

What are your particular areas of expertise or interest?

My clinical and research interests are related to minority health and health disparities. Specific areas of expertise include behavioral interventions for pediatric sickle-cell disease and child/adolescent nutrition and obesity.

Describe your employment setting and the activities in which you engage? How do you spend your days?

I am an Assistant Professor (tenure-track) in the Department of Health Behavior at the University of Alabama at Birmingham School of Public Health. Like most other faculty at major universities, I spend my time engaged in teaching, scholarly activities (research and publications), and service (participating on working groups, committees, etc.; presenting at conferences/meetings; grant reviews).

Most days I:

- work on one of three currently funded research grants to develop and test interventions to improve child and adolescent health

  - assist with participant recruitment

  - develop intervention curricula

  - supervise project staff

  - review project expenditures

  - attend project team meetings

  - ensure treatment fidelity for projects (e.g., review audio/video tapes of intervention sessions to ensure that the intervention is appropriately administered)

  - review data analysis

- advise M.P.H. and Ph.D. students and serve on graduate dissertation committees

- prepare for or teach a course (graduate level)

- work on a grant application (to fund research) or manuscript

What are the advantages and disadvantages of your career choice and setting? What should students know in considering such a career?

Advantages:

- Public health, particularly focusing on minority health and health disparities, is a timely topic.

- I get to see how my programs/ideas can be used to impact numbers of people at once (hopefully in a positive way).

- Work in an academic setting (particularly a research institution) allows for a great deal of flexibility in my work schedule and the types of activities that I get involved in (not just one thing over and over again).

- Because I am licensed (and keep it current), I have additional options for employment beyond my current work.

- I can influence the training of future psychologists and public health practitioners/scientists.

- There a number of other professionals with my interests that I can collaborate with.

- There are a number of resources at a major research institution to assist me in getting research funding and publications.

- Relative to others I know working in more "traditional" settings for psychologists; the salaries of psychologists in public health settings are higher.

Disadvantages:
- The education and training it took to get me to my current job took a long time (4 years for B.A.; 2 years for M.S.; 5 years for Ph.D.; 1 year postdoc; 3 years in nontenure track faculty position).

- Tenure-track faculty positions require a high level of self-motivation, tenacity, and many hours working. In order to reach tenure at a major research university, one has to be extremely productive (publication, grantsmanship, national/international services, teaching).

- There are limited opportunities to work with individuals in public health settings. I sometimes miss working with individual clients/patients and their families.

- I sometimes feel that to be optimally effective in my current position, I should go back to school for a M.P.H.

Students should consider:
- The length of education/training needed to be competitive for jobs in public health.

- Whether they enjoy impacting lots of people at a minimal level (more like public health) or fewer people with greater intensity (more like individual therapy/counseling).

- Whether the demands of tenure-track faculty position are consistent with their personality/interest.

How can students prepare themselves for such a career?

- Take courses in health psychology and/or public health (e.g., epidemiology, health behavior).

- Talk with faculty in public health, particularly those in departments such as health behavior or behavioral science.

- Talk with students in public health, particularly those in departments such as health behavior or behavioral science

- Identify health-related areas of interest.

- Identify researchers with similar interest and inquire about assistant-ships or research supplements from the faculty member's work.

The above will assist students in determining whether they are committed to the investment that it will take to be successful in this type of career. They will also provide opportunities for research experience, grant writing, and/or presentations and publication (any of which will help the student stand out from the crowd when applying for graduate school). They will also begin to network with potential mentors, advisors, and/or employers.

Profile 3.3: APA's Congressional and Executive Branch Fellowship Program

More than half of the 2002–2003 participants in APA's Congressional and Executive Branch Fellowship Program plan to pursue policy-related careers after the experience.

"It's like an adult Disneyland," says congressional fellow Neil Kirschner, Ph.D., of his legislative duties on Capitol Hill, which include drafting speeches on innovative topics—on breakneck deadlines—and attending briefings on cutting-edge research topics. Kirschner, who is among those who have caught the policy bug, adds, "There are all kinds of intellectually challenging adventures every day."

Through the congressional fellowships, the Science Policy Fellowship Program and the Practice Organization's Health Policy Fellowship, APA places psychologists in congressional offices and in executive branch research and mental health service agencies to learn about policy-making first-hand and to increase the visibility of psychologists in the policy process. Fellows work in the nation's capital from September through August, with financial support from APA. Here's a glimpse at the accomplishments of the most recent crop of fellows.

Enhancing welfare

The possibility of leaving her mark on welfare reauthorization drew congressional fellow Cathy Cozzarelli, Ph.D., out of academe to work for Sen. Jeff Bingaman (D-N.M.), a member of the Senate Health, Education, Labor and Pensions Committee that oversees welfare.

"I had worked on social issues for years," says Cozzarelli, a professor of psychology at Kansas State University, of her research on issues such as post-abortion adjustment and attitudes toward the poor. "But before, it always felt like I was having minimal world impact."

On Capitol Hill, she can already see ways that her work may bring about social change. She helped draft a bill to increase the amount of child-care money available to lower-income workers and another to create government-funded transitional jobs for people with barriers to regular employment—such as victims of domestic violence and workers who can't read or write well. She is particularly encouraged about her contributions to two new child-care and welfare bills that would enable American Indian tribes to access federal funds to set up their own child-care or welfare programs.

"We are also trying to make it easier for them to construct facilities—reservations often have terrible conditions; they don't have the infrastructure and buildings that states take for granted," says Cozzarelli.

Cozzarelli says the fellowship has taught her how to capture policy-makers' attention with her future research. "If you are interested in doing that, this fellowship is the best tutorial you can get," she says.

Battling spam

Congressional fellow Linda Demaine, J.D., Ph.D., has spent her fellowship year working for the Senate Judiciary Committee. She has conducted FBI and Department of Justice oversight work, including questioning the legality of the FBI's recent request for information from educational institutions on foreign students and teachers, and participating in a bipartisan effort by the committee to protect an FBI whistleblower from retaliation within the bureau.

Demaine has also conducted background investigations on judicial nominees, the results of which are used by committee members when deciding whether to support or oppose the nominations. She initiated the involvement of ranking committee member Sen. Patrick Leahy (D-Vt.) in developing and gathering support for anti-spam legislation, and is involved with drafting legislation she describes as "a narrow anti-spam bill that targets perhaps the most egregious spamming practices, routing spam through someone else's computer or falsifying the routing information or identity in order to make it look as though the message came from that other person."

Demaine, who took a year off for the fellowship from her position as a behavioral scientist at RAND, says the Capitol Hill experience has been enlightening.

"Seeing first-hand the inner workings of Congress can be simultaneously disconcerting and empowering," says Demaine. "While scientific findings, and even the public interest, are not often given the weight they deserve, psychologists who understand the legislative process are in a better position to communicate effectively with Congress and thereby influence policy."

Bolstering science and math education

Science policy fellow Tamara Jackson, Ph.D., is working to improve science and math education in her post at the White House's Office of Science and Technology Policy (OSTP).

"There is a significant concern about the quality of math and science education that our youth are receiving, particularly regarding the issue of teacher preparation," says Jackson, adding that interest in science and math is waning among youth and fewer of them are pursuing degrees in science and engineering fields. "This creates a significant concern of whether there will be a generation that is well-prepared and qualified to meet the future demands of the science and engineering work-force."

To create a solution, Jackson is working with a subcommittee of the National Science and Technology Council that links government agencies with a stake in science and math education—including the Department of Energy, Department of Defense, the National Science Foundation (NSF) and NASA. Together they will take stock of their science and math education programs, identify training gaps and create new research and development initiatives, says Jackson. She's also participating in a joint effort with the NSF and the Department of Education to create new ways to spark children's and teenagers' interest in math and science. The effort will draw on research on what boosts learning in these areas and will include national campaigns to spotlight the need for better math and science education and to recruit, prepare and retain teachers with strong math and science backgrounds.

The OSTP fellowship is Jackson's second in the nation's capital: Last year she held Catherine Cozzarelli's position in Bingaman's office and pursued this next fellowship to test the waters in the executive branch. Her next move? Hopefully a permanent position in health policy, she says.

Guiding health-care policy

Congressional fellow Neil Kirschner, Ph.D., was charged with no small task when he began his fellowship: Bring at least five bills to the floor of the House of Representatives. Kirschner, who works on health-care issues exclusively and splits his time between the Subcommittee on Health of the House Ways and Means Committee and its ranking member Rep. Pete Stark (D-Calif.), has already accomplished that goal.

He has, for example, helped introduce legislation that would award families of organ donors a Congressional Gift of Life Medal—to help encourage organ donation—as well as legislation that would modernize Medicare and a bill to compensate social workers for providing mental health services in nursing homes. He is particularly hopeful about improving Medicare, which hasn't been significantly updated since it came into effect in 1965. He recently discovered data from the Substance Abuse and Mental Health Services Administration (SAMHSA) showing that higher-than-average Medicare co-payments for outpatient mental health services actually lead to increased inpatient costs. "Beneficiaries are not seeking outpatient treatment because it is too expensive, so it leads them to overuse the hospital setting," Kirschner says. He is working to change that Medicare policy.

Although he previously spent more than 20 years as a clinical psychologist and administrator at the Taylor Manor Hospital and Health System in Ellicott City, Md., Kirschner plans to transition to a job in health policy or government relations when the fellowship ends. He encourages APA members to make his next job easier by getting more involved in politics and writing to their members of Congress.

"People have no idea that constituent letters are like gold here," he says.

Aiding impoverished countries

A desire to help underserved populations led Congressional Fellow Mischa Thompson, Ph.D., to the office of Rep. Charles B. Rangel (D-N.Y.).

She's had the opportunity to work in depth on one of Rangel's main priorities: boosting the socioeconomic status of impoverished countries in the Caribbean, South America and Africa. Thompson is examining ways to enhance U.S. foreign policy and trade initiatives so funds get to the people who need them most. She has worked on President Bush's $15 billion global AIDS bill that targets the Caribbean, and has worked to direct U.S. foreign aid to impoverished Afro-Latino communities in South America. Also on her radar screen are the negotiations of the U.S.–Central America Free Trade Agreement. She is working to include provisions that will provide economic development opportunities for impoverished indigenous and Afro-Latino populations in Guatemala, Honduras, El Salvador, Nicaragua and Costa Rica.

The fellowship is Thompson's first job since earning her Ph.D. in social psychology from the University of Michigan, Ann Arbor. She became interested in policy there when, as the student chair of the Society for the Psychological

Study of Social Issues, she met former APA congressional fellows. That exposure led her to organize sessions at APA's Annual Convention where students could talk with policy experts and to pursue the fellowship.

Thompson foresees a long-term career in public policy. When she completes her fellowship she'll begin work as a Science Policy Fellow in an executive branch agency through APA's Public Policy Office.

Scrutinizing managed care

Longtime private practitioner William Wallace, Ph.D., is learning the ins and outs of managed care as the Health Policy Fellow in the Office of Organization and Financing of the Center for Mental Health Services, part of SAMHSA.

Wallace edits research and analysis reports written by health policy economists, preparing them for publication by identifying any gaps in content or methodological problems. He's reviewed an upcoming report on the effects of the Vermont parity law on health-care access and costs and another on states' use of medical necessity in utilization review in determining levels of insurance coverage. He is also drafting a report on the costs associated with the Colorado parity law.

"It has been a fascinating experience to get an overall view of what is happening across all the states and an understanding of how managed care really works in terms of its economics," says Wallace. "It's not really managed care, its managing costs and how they go about doing that."

When his fellowship ends, Wallace will return home to Santa Monica, Calif., in search of a new career at a think tank or nonprofit organization that influences state policy-making. It won't be his first career shift: Wallace was an Episcopal priest before he became a psychologist, and has been a non-stipendary priest for more than 35 years. In fact, his spirituality inspired his interest in policy.

"Part of the reason I am so interested in increasing access to mental health is that I believe we have a real moral responsibility to help people," he says.

(Reprinted with permission from Chamberlian, 2003.)

PSYCHOLOGISTS IN THE MILITARY

CHAPTER GUIDE

ACTIVITIES OF PSYCHOLOGISTS IN THE MILITARY

PERSONNEL SELECTION AND CLASSIFICATION

PERSONNEL TRAINING

LEADERSHIP AND TEAM EFFECTIVENESS

DIRECT SERVICE

ADVANTAGES, DISADVANTAGES, AND SALARY

PREPARATION FOR A CAREER IN THE MILITARY

RECOMMENDED READINGS

WEB RESOURCES

PROFILE 4.1: CARRIE M. DORSON, PSY.D.

One employment setting that clinical and counseling psychologists often over-look is the military. Over 800 psychologists are employed by the military (Careers in the Military, n.d.) and more than 500 are active-duty clinical and counseling psychologists (Johnson, 2002). The military offers a range of enlisted and civilian opportunities for psychologists. In this chapter we examine the activities and roles in which clinical and counseling psychologists perform, including personnel selection and classification, training, leadership and team effectiveness, and direct service (American Psychological Association; n.d.; Wisckoff, 1997).

ACTIVITIES OF PSYCHOLOGISTS IN THE MILITARY

Military psychology is defined by the context of application: the military (Driskell & Olmstead, 1989). Psychologists work to promote the "fighting power and combat readiness of individual personnel and the military collective". (Page, 1996, p. 383). That entails a variety of activities, as we'll discuss in the following sections.

Personnel Selection and Classification

The success of the military relies on the ability to quickly and accurately select, train, and motivate people to undertake difficult and complicated assignments in frequently life-threatening circumstances (Johnson, 2002). Psychologists screen, select, and place recruits, eliminating those who are not suitable on the basis of psychological impairment. They also select personnel for jobs requiring special skills such as piloting aircraft, air traffic control, and special operations personnel. Personnel who volunteer or are recommended for leadership positions are evaluated thoroughly because leadership assignments are particularly stressful and a poor personnel choice can cost lives (Page, 1996). Psychologists create procedures for evaluating the performance of enlisted and officer personnel and conduct research on how to use simulators to evaluate special abilities.

Personnel Training

Psychologists work to develop effective and efficient means of training personnel and increasing operational readiness (American Psychological Association; n.d.). They conduct research examining the most effective techniques of training personnel in basic skills (e.g., reading, mathematics), military skills (e.g., seamanship), and technical skills (e.g., electronics), as well as how to increase operational readiness. They conduct research on how to design effective instructional systems, measure training performance, and best use technology in training, such as computer-simulated scenarios and virtual reality. Psychologists study how to help military personnel operate most efficiently, maintain health, enhance performance, and reduce human error under adverse circumstances, including sleep deprivation, extreme environmental conditions, and hazardous conditions.

Psychologists provide their expertise in designing and monitoring special training, such as Survival Evasion Resistance Escape (SERE) training. The purpose of SERE training, is to prepare individuals who are at high risk of being captured as a POW and to protect national security (Souter, 2002). SERE training entails teaching trainees ways to avoid compromising themselves or their country. During simulated capture and interrogation sessions, trainees learn what to do and how to manage themselves in dangerous and anxiety-provoking situations. The psychologist's role is to educate trainers about the psychological dynamics of hostage and POW situations and to monitor the training sessions to ensure that the simulations are powerful enough to have an impact, but not too extreme as to harm trainees (Smith, 2002). Trainees learn counter-interrogation methods to avoid giving away important information, how to cope with isolation, sleep deprivation, and despair, and how to deal with the fear of what may be coming next. Clearly, psychologists have a special role in designing, implementing, and monitoring special training.

Leadership and Team Effectiveness

Some psychologists study team effectiveness and how to improve communication in multinational forces. Psychologists study how to promote effective leadership as well as how to select, train, and evaluate leaders. They apply research findings in their work with leaders, helping the leaders to be more effective by teaching leadership techniques as well as explaining cultural differences that influence communication styles. Psychologists examine and work to improve team processes such as communication, subordinate-supervisor relations, team cohesion, the functioning of small groups, and tactical decision making. Psychologists' expertise in understanding and promoting group functioning as well as their ability to coach leaders and team members is valued.

Direct Service

Clinical and counseling psychologists in the military often work in counseling or mental health clinics providing mental health services, counseling, and psychoeducational instruction to improve the lives of military personnel and their families. Counseling and clinical psychologists serve in a wide variety of direct service settings such as military hospitals, outpatient clinics, mental health centers, day care centers, military prisons, and onboard ships.

Psychologists assist reservists in coping with the transition to active duty. They help personnel acclimate to military life, deal with stress, anxiety, and depression, diagnose pathology, and cope with serious psychological reactions in the aftermath of combat. Although the direct service activities of clinical and counseling psychologists in the military are similar to those of civilians, mental health may have a more profound impact in a military setting (Souter, 2002). For example, consider someone who loads or handles nuclear weapons; a psychologists' erroneous judgment of his or her emotional stability holds grave implications. Psychologists also help service members understand and process traumatic events. For example, they provide "critical event debriefings after any exceptionally stressful situation such as the death of a unit member. The debriefing allows members to talk about what happened, correct any misperceptions about the event, discuss lessons learned and find out how to get help if they continue to feel anxious" (Rabasca, 2000).

Increasingly, psychologists are assigned to aircraft carriers because they are stressful places and a psychologist's presence has been shown to reduce the number of sailors evacuated from warships and sent back to shore for psychological evaluations, saving both money and work hours (Mattas-Curry, 1999). Psychologists also join the front lines to treat service members for combat stress. When service members are treated as close to the operational front as possible with the expectation that they will go back on duty, they usually recover more quickly than when they're evacuated from the combat zone (Mattas-Curry, 1999). The prevention activities of psychologists help soldiers learn how to deal with stress and avoid posttraumatic reactions; psychologists also offer stress inoculation before service members go overseas.

In addition to therapeutic activities, psychologists conduct fitness-for-duty assessments to determine whether personnel are emotionally and psychologically fit. Psychologists also develop and implement programs to help service members reduce stress; wellness; and deal with common issues like substance abuse (American Psychological Association; n.d.).

ADVANTAGES, DISADVANTAGES, AND SALARY

Many psychologists conduct their work as civilians in military and V.A. hospitals. If you choose a career in the military, your doctoral degree will confer officer status. As a clinical or counseling psychologist in the military, you have the opportunity to make a difference in the lives of service personnel and their families, in the operation of the military at large, and ultimately, in the stability of our nation and the world (American Psychological Association; n.d.).

Psychologists in the military often spend significant amounts of time overseas which, depending on your inclination and family situation, may be an advantage or disadvantage. Clinical and counseling psychologists go wherever there are concentrations of troops, in peacetime and war, and to hostile environments. A uniformed psychologist can count on a change of geographical location every 2 to 3 years (Wiskoff, 1997). Despite the wear and tear of travel on relationships with family and friends, the military psychologists' opportunities to see the world are unmatched. In addition to travel commitments, uniformed psychologists must pass fitness tests (as is required of all service members) and wear uniforms.

An important drawback of practicing psychology in a military setting is the absence of confidentiality in the therapeutic relationship. Members of the military who seek or are referred for mental health services do not have the same rights and privileges to confidentiality that nonmilitary clients enjoy. Rather, higher-ranking personnel may and do request information regarding the functioning of service members. In effect, the government is the client and psychologists' first responsibility is to aid the military in defending the country; other responsibilities are secondary (Johnson, 2002). A variety of ethical issues arise when clinical and counseling psychologists practice in military settings. Psychologists, thus, must manage professional dilemmas such as balancing respect for individual clients with the potential need to disclose confidential information (Johnson, 2002).

No discussion of the advantages and disadvantages of a career in the military would be complete without exploring the challenges that active duty entails, including the potential for living and working in a war zone. In addition to the stress of managing one's own safety and welfare, psychologists must assist service members in managing their conflicting emotions and fears. Military psychologists sometimes feel burdened with responsibility because their role is to help service members maintain their focus on their jobs and perform well. "Psychologists have to be the cheerleaders and confessors, taking care of individuals psychologically so that their minds, bodies and spirits are ready to do the hard jobs they'll be asked to do" (Clay, 2001). The burden of responsibility is also felt when psychologists must make decisions about an individual's fitness for duty or for special assignment. These decisions have vast implications for the lives and careers of service members.

Finally, once you join the ranks and become an officer in the military, there is no "changing your mind." You must serve for the duration of your commitment. Consider your own needs and satisfaction with the military lifestyle, because once you are sworn in as an officer, you can't simply quit and try another career. The military, however, offers important benefits, including job security, opportunities for additional education, and an excellent benefits and retirement system. Few professional positions offer the opportunity to retire after as few as 20 years of service, and to do so with a pension. The salary scale for military psychologists is aligned with the government pay scales but with some very important benefits (Wiskoff, 1997). In 2001, government starting salary for doctoral level psychologists was $40,200 (Bureau of Labor Statistics, 2002). In addition to a base salary, the amount of which depends on your rank and pay rate (doctoral-level psychologists enter the military as officers), military personnel get subsistence and housing allowances, which are not taxable. All officers receive about $160 per month substistence pay; the housing allowance varies depending on where you are stationed (i.e., cost of living) and whether you have dependents.

For example, consider this sample housing allowance in several areas around the United States:
- St. Louis, MO = $985 for single and $1,124 for married
- New London, CT = $1,282 for single and $1,494 for married
- San Diego, CA = $ 1,598 for single and $1,905 for married
- Washington DC = $1,635 for single and = $2,072 for married
- San Francisco, CA = $2,540 for single and $2,944 for married

Clearly, there are significant financial benefits associated with entering the military.

PREPARATION FOR A CAREER IN THE MILITARY

If you're interested in a clinical or counseling psychology career in the military, seek broad training experiences in addition to your clinical or counseling psychology studies. Specifically, develop skills as a generalist: the ability to practice under varied circumstances and with a wide variety of client populations is highly valued (Johnson & Wilson, 1993). Seek additional training and experience in consultation and community psychology and "brief clinical interventions with an emphasis on assessment, diagnosis, and intervention in a single session" (Johnson & Wilson, 1993, p. 313). Courses in forensic psychology and police psychology will help you learn valuable skills, such as hostage negotiation (Souter, 2002). A thorough understanding of stress responses, coping strategies, emotional management techniques, and health promotion strategies will prepare you for meeting the needs of service members. Applied training in organizational development and leadership will round out your skills (Johnson, 2002). Moreover, hone your communication skills; the ability to communicate well orally and in writing is essential. Learn how to present information concisely and in visual format because a great deal of communication in the military is conducted through group briefings in which you'll have a few minutes to get your message across to people of many different backgrounds, skill levels, and educations.

Consider a military predoctoral or postdoctoral internship, residency, or fellowship. There are a variety of opportunities for active-duty service members and some for civilian psychologists. Military internships offer unique opportunities. For example, military stipends are among the highest in the country (Johnson & Wilson, 1993). Such internships challenge the limits of one's physical and emotional abilities and are adventurous. For example, Johnson and Wilson (1993) describe their experiences as interns at Bethesda Naval Hospital in which they were indoctrinated to military service, completed Officer Indoctrination School, toured submarines and an aircraft carrier, and through completing four distinct clinical rotations, received excellent training and honed solid generalist skills. For more information about military internships, residencies, and fellowships, consult the resources in Table 4.1.

TABLE 4.1   MILITARY INTERNSHIPS, RESIDENCIES, AND FELLOWSHIPS FOR PSYCHOLOGISTS

Brooke Army Medical Center: Clinical Psychology Residency Program
http://www.bamc.amedd.army.mil/Beh%20Med%20Brochure.html

Clinical Psychology Internship Program of the U.S. Navy
http://www.bethesda.med.navy.mil/external/Clinical_Psychology_Internship_Program.pdf

Clinical Psychology Internships in the US Navy
http://www-nmcp.mar.med.navy.mil/Psychology/all.asp

Eisenhower Army Medical Center: Clinical Psychology Residency Training
http://www.ddeamc.amedd.army.mil/Clinical/MentalHealth/Psychology/PsyResid.htm

Fellowship Training Program
http://www.whmc.af.mil/Psychology/fellowship/index.htm

Tripler Army Medical Center: Clinical Psychology Residency Program
http://www.tamc.amedd.army.mil/residency/mchk-ph/cprp.htm

Tripler Army Medical Center: Postdoctoral Fellowship in Clinical Psychology
http://www.tamc.amedd.army.mil/residency/mchk-ph/pfpp.htm

Walter Reed Army Medical Center: Psychology Training Programs
http://www.wramc.amedd.army.mil/departments/psychology/trainingindex.htm

U.S. Army Clinical Psychology Residency Programs
http://www.ddeamc.amedd.army.mil/Clinical/MentalHealth/Psychology/Army%20C
PRP%20Brochure%202003-2004%20Revision%202.pdf

Willford Hall Medical Center: Clinical Psychology Residency (Internship) Program
http://www.whmc.af.mil/Psychology/residency/index.htm

Finally, before committing yourself to enter the military, carefully consider the implications of your choice. Clarify your preferences, both personal and professional. Determine your short- and long-term goals. Identify your core values, strengths, and weaknesses. Question your attitudes toward military service and authority. Consider your geographic preferences as well as the implications of separation from your family. Take the time that you need to determine your willingness and ability to commit to a minimum 3 years of active service. Military service—and careers in the military—offer many opportunities but also entail great responsibility.

RECOMMENDED READINGS

Friedlander, J. N. (in press). An army clinical psychologist. In R. D. Morgan, T. L. Kuther, & C. J. Habben (Eds.), *Life after graduate school: Advice from new psychologists.* New York: Psychology Press.

Gal, R. A., Mangelsdorff, D. A., & Dolgin, D. L. (1996). *Handbook of military psychology.* New York: Wiley.

Johnson, W. B., & Wilson, K. (1993). The military internship: A retrospective analysis. *Professional Psychology: Research and Practice, 24,* 312–318.

McGuire, F. (1990). *Psychology aweigh! A history of clinical psychology in the United States Navy.* Washington, DC: American Psychological Assocaition.

Page, G. D. (1996). Clinical psychology in the military: Developments and issues. *Clinical Psychology Review, 16,* 383–396

Wiskoff, M. F. (1997). Defense of the nation: Military psychologists. In R. J. Sternberg (Ed.), *Career paths in psychology: Where your degree can take you* (pp. 245–268). Washington, DC: American Psychological Association.

WEB RESOURCES

About the U.S. Military
   http://usmilitary.about.com/
APA Division 19—Military Psychology
   http://www.apa.org/division/div19.html
United States Army
   http://www.army.mil/
United States Air Force
   http://www.af.mil/
United States Navy
   http://www.navy.mil/
United States Marines
   http://www.usmc.mil/

PROFILE 4.1: CARRIE DORSON, PSY.D.

Dr. Carrie M. Dorson is Chief of Psychological Services at the Life Skills Support Center, Ellsworth Air Force Base, and an active duty Air Force Officer. She is licensed in the state of Alabama. She received her B.A.S. in psychology with a minor in women's studies from the University of Minnesota, M.A. in clinical psychology from Minnesota School of Professional Psychology, and Psy.D. in clinical psychology from Minnesota School of Professional Psychology. She completed her predoctoral internship at Tripler Army Medical Center in Honolulu, Hawaii, and served 4 years on active duty as United States Army psychologist prior to her commission into the United States Air Force. Dr. Dotson has been in the Air Force for 1 year. I asked Dr. Dorson about her experiences in psychology in the military.

Describe your background. How did you become interested in psychology?

I completed my undergraduate training at the University of Minnesota with a degree in psychology a minor in women's studies. I immediately began graduate school through the Minnesota School of Professional Psychology (MSPP), which is now named Argosy University. MSPP is a professional school leading to a doctorate in clinical psychology or a Psy.D. degree. I began graduate school part time before deciding this was what I wanted to do and earned my master's degree and doctorate degree in 5 years.

The requirement for a doctorate degree in clinical psychology is to complete an internship during the student's fourth year of school. I applied to both civilian and military internship sites. I was selected for a United States Army internship in Honolulu, Hawaii, at Tripler Army Medical Center. The military sites appealed to me because of their long-standing programs, APA accreditation, commitment to training, resources, and pat! I served for 4 years in the Army before my commitment was complete. At that time, I applied for a commission in the Air Force and am currently serving on active duty as a psychologist for the Air Force.

I became interested in psychology and working with people in high school. I was very active in 4-H, and in particular, I was active in child development programs. I considered medical school and physical therapy as career options, but when I started college, I had not decided on a specific career. After completing some college courses psychology, I decided to pursue my undergraduate degree in psychology. As I was getting ready to graduate, I learned that an undergraduate degree in psychology doesn't mean much and if I wanted to become a psychologist. I needed to get my doctorate.

What are your particular area of expertise or interest?

I am considered a generalist in clinical psychology. My particular area of interest is pediatric psychology and my goal is to complete a fellowship, which would entail 1–2 more years of training.

Describe your employment setting and the activities in which you engage. How do you spend your days?

I work in a small medical clinic that includes a primary care clinic as well as dental, optometry, physical therapy, and a mental health clinic. Our clinic has four military providers (two psychologists and two social workers) as well as several civilian social workers. We have four enlisted mental health technicians and one civilian secretary. Our services include individual and group therapy through the mental health section. Our social work section provides family maltreatment-support, new parent support, and alcohol and and drug treatment.

My primary job is chief of the psychological services and I supervise one unlicensed psychologist as well as the mental health technicians who are trained to do initial evaluations of patients. I provide mostly individual therapy to active-duty service members, but provide some marital counseling and group counseling to service members and their families. I spend one half-day a week working in the primary care clinic as a consultant to the medical providers for depression, anxiety, sleep and health-related problems. I also conduct prevention classes for service members who are unable to meet the physical fitness standards.

What are the advantages and disadvantages of your career choice and setting? What should students know in considering such a career?

The advantages of my career-choice include the following: exciting and diverse job possibilities, frequent moves to new locations including overseas assignments, guaranteed job and supervision for licensure, good pay and benefits, funding for conferences, support of over 200 Air Force psychologists to utilize as resources, opportunity to complete a fellowship, and loan repayment programs.

Some might consider these as disadvantages: signing a commitment to serve in the military for 3–4 years, serving as an active-duty service member who could be deployed to a hostile area, wearing a uniform and following military rules and regulations.

How can students prepare themselves for such a career?

The best way to prepare for a career in the military is to obtain a broad base of clinical experiences as it is not unusual for a psychologist to obtain a first assignment to a base where he/she is the only psychologist and in charge of a clinic. Also, military assignments can be physically demanding. Psychologists in the military need to be able to meet height and weight standards as well as pass a physical fitness test. In addition, psychologists can be deployed to locations that are extreme in temperatures and conditions so it is important to be physically fit. Students who are preparing for a military career should be physically active.

FORENSIC AND POLICE PSYCHOLOGY CAREERS

CHAPTER GUIDE

FORENSIC PSYCHOLOGY

ACTIVITIES OF FORENSIC
PSYCHOLOGISTS

ADVANTAGES AND DISADVANTAGES
OF A CAREER IN FORENSIC
PSYCHOLOGY

PREPARATION FOR A CAREER IN
FORENSIC PSYCHOLOGY

POLICE PSYCHOLOGY

ACTIVITIES OF POLICE
PSYCHOLOGISTS

ADVANTAGES AND DISADVANTAGES
TO A CAREER IN POLICE
PSYCHOLOGY

PREPARATION FOR A CAREER IN
POLICE PSYCHOLOGY

RECOMMENDED READINGS

WEB RESOURCES

**PROFILE 5.1: KAREN FRANKLIN,
PH.D.**

**PROFILE 5.2: EVAN NELSON,
PH.D.**

**PROFILE 5.3: ELLEN
KIRCHMAN, PH.D.**

**PROFILE 5.4: GARY KAUFMANN,
PSY.D.**

Called to the scene of the crime, the psychologist creates a profile of the criminal by examining the clues left at the crime scene. Explaining the ramifications of each clue left behind, the psychologist provides the homicide detectives with an overview of the offender's personality and characteristics that will aid in his or her pursuit and capture. Certainly this represents the work of forensic and police psychologists, right?

Popular films and television shows like *Silence of the Lambs*, *CSI*, and *Profiler* depict psychologists' work in forensic and police arenas as action-packed careers. Such portrayals emphasize psychologists' activities in profiling dangerous criminals; however, few forensic psychologists actually engage in criminal profiling. Popular press and media portrayals contribute to beliefs that forensic and police psychology careers make for exciting TV-like action-adventures, but this is rarely the case (Kuther, 2004). So then, what do police and forensic psychologists do?.

Forensic Psychology

What is forensic psychology? The American Board of Forensic Psychology and the American Psychology-Law Society (1995) define forensic psychology as:

> the professional practice by psychologists within the areas of clinical psychology, counseling psychology, neuropsychology, and school psychology, when they are engaged regularly as experts and represent themselves as such, in an activity primarily intended to provide professional psychological expertise to the judicial system. (p. 6).

In other words, forensic psychology refers to the practice of psychological assessment and treatment activities within a legal setting.

Some have argued that this definition of forensic psychology is too narrow because it limits the scope of forensic psychology to practice-related issues, such as assessing cognitive competence, determining a defendant's mental state at the time of the crime, and other activities that require training in clinical or counseling psychology (Wrightsman, 2001). Critics point out that psychologists engage in other activities that intersect with the legal system, such as evaluation-research, trial consulting and non–assessment-based expert testimony. Nevertheless, the more narrow practice-related definition of forensic psychology, posed by the American Board of Forensic Psychology and the American Psychology-Law Society, has been accepted and conferred specialty status by the American Psychological Association (APA), meaning that graduate training programs can now seek specialty designations as forensic psychology programs (American Psychological Association, 2001).

Activities of Forensic Psychologists

Forensic psychologists conduct psychological evaluations of individuals in both criminal and civil court cases. They write comprehensive reports documenting their findings in order to inform the court about important psychological issues that hold implications for the trial, such as a defendant's mental state at the time of the crime, whether a defendant is competent for trial, or whether a plaintiff's injuries suggest malingering (falsification). Some forensic reports are requested by (and delivered to) the court, others, the client, and the attorney. In some jurisdictions, the psychologist must attend court to and answer questions about it in order for the report to be considered courtroom evidence (Walker, 1990).

- **Criminal Cases** Criminal court cases are those in which an individual has committed a crime against society (Huss, 2001). Psychologists might be called on in criminal cases to provide testimo ny on the following kinds of issues:

- **Adjudicative Competence** Forensic psychologists commonly are asked to assess adjudicative competence, or the defendant's capacity to understand the legal proceedings and function meaningfully within the court setting (Wrightsman et al., 2002). Is the defendant competent to stand trial? Is the defendant able to plead guilty and waive his or her constitutional rights, such as the right to a jury trial? Does the defendant have the capacity to waive his or her right to an attorney and instead represent him- or herself at trial?

- **Criminal Responsibility** Was the defendant aware of the implications of his or her actions at the time of the offense? Does the defendant suffer from psychological problems that may have influenced the crime? For example, consider a criminal case in which a defendant who has been diagnosed with schizophrenia is accused of murder. A forensic psychologist might be called on to conduct an evaluation to determine whether the person's judgment and impulse control was impaired by his or her diagnosis at the time of the crime.

- **Victim Trauma and Injury** Forensic psychologists frequently play a role in evaluating the effects of trauma or injuries on victims. A forensic psychologist may evaluate a victim of violent crime to determine trauma symptoms, document psychological functioning before and after the crime, and determine social adjustment and coping after the assault.

- **Veracity of Child Abuse Allegations** Forensic psychologists interview children who allege physical or sexual abuse to determine their ability to testify. The content of children's reports may be examined to distinguish truthful allegations from fantasy, and the results are reported to the court.

Civil Cases In a civil court case, an individual brings forth a suit to resolve a dispute between two parties or because they believe that someone has physically or emotionally injured them (Huss, 2001). Forensic psychologists aid civil cases by providing the following types of evaluations:

- **Child Custody Evaluations** Child custody cases are among the fastest growing areas of forensic psychological assessment. In these cases, forensic psychologists interview and assess families to make a recommendation regarding the custodial arrangement that is in the best interests of the child whose parents are divorcing.

- **Competency Evaluations** Forensic psychologists assess the decisional competence of individuals. Is the older adult competent to prepare a will or to manage his or her financial affairs? Can the adolescent make reasoned decisions regarding medical or psychiatric treatment? Is the individual able to draw up a living will?

- **Civil Commitment** Is the individual a danger to him- or herself? Does he or she require hospitalization for mental health treatment? Is the individual dangerous to others? Must the individual receive mandatory mental health treatment within an outpatient setting? Answering each of these questions requires a forensic evaluation.

- **Psychological Damages** Civil court cases often involve plaintiffs who seek compensation for psychological injuries caused by a second party, including emotional distress, posttraumatic stress disorder, and depression. For example, consider a parent who has witnessed the death of a child due to negligence on the part of an individual or company (e.g., an amusement ride accident caused by lack of regular maintenance). The parent may sue the individual or company to provide financial compensation for the emotional and psychological trauma that he or she has experienced. Forensic psychologists also provide evaluations within the context of workers' compensation cases. Workers who suffer serious physical injuries that leave them with chronic pain often demonstrate psychological symptoms like anxiety and depression. In each of these examples, a forensic psychologist might conduct an evaluation to determine the extent of emotional or psychological trauma.

- **Psychological Autopsy** Psychological autopsies are uncommon and entail providing an evaluation of the deceased person's state of mind before death (Shneidman, 1994). For example, was the individual competent to create or modify a will before death? Was the death a homicide, suicide, or accident? Clearly, psychological autopsies are unusual and challenging evaluations in which conclusions cannot be stated with certainty (Shneidman, 1994). In fact the overall validity of psychological autopsies has been challenged (Selkin, 1994).

Forensic psychologists engage in many forms of evaluation. Many work in private practice, and some criminal forensic psychologists work in state institutions, such as secure forensic units, community mental health centers, and hospitals, where they conduct risk assessments of offenders and other at-risk individuals before they are released (Kuther, 2004).

Advantages and Disadvantages of a Career in Forensic Psychology

The primary advantages of forensic psychology include intellectual stimulation, job satisfaction in helping to serve society, as well as the potential to earn a comfortable income. Entry-level psychologists providing forensic services in hospitals and community settings may begin at approximately $50,000 annually, but salaries tend to vary by state and jurisdiction (American Psychology-Law Society, 1998). Forensic psychologists in private practice typically bill between $150 and $250 per hour, but must work hard at making a steady income. It is difficult to predict ups and downs in a private practice, so financial planning and marketing or promotion of one's services is essential, as we discussed in Chapter 2.

An important disadvantage of a career in forensic psychology is the potential for lawsuits and ethics complaints filed against forensic examiners. Those who specialize in child custody and child abuse cases are especially likely to experience board complaints and ethics charges; it has been estimated that 7–10% of ethics complaints reported to the American Psychological Association are against child custody evaluators (Glassman, 1998). Fortunately, frivolous cases tend to be dismissed quickly; only 1% of psychologists charged ethics complaints receive discipline (Kirkland & Kirkland, 2001). However, even frivolous lawsuits or ethics complaints can be costly in terms of finances, time, stress, and professional image. Needless to say, forensic psychologists may experience considerable stress even without the threat of complaints or lawsuits because many court cases, especially child custody cases, are highly emotional for all parties.

Although forensic psychologists often write forensic evaluations that inform the court, sometimes they are asked to supplement their reports with testimony or to provide testimony as a pure expert—that is, to discuss the scientific evidence regarding a particular question or phenomena. The opportunity to provide courtroom testimony may be an advantage or disadvantage to a career in forensic psychology, depending on your education, experience, and taste for the confrontative nature of legal challenges (Hess, 1998; Lloyd-Bostock, 1988). The cross examination may challenge your education, training, competence, and the validity and reliability of forensic assessment.

Preparation for a Career in Forensic Psychology

Students who seek careers in forensic psychology should seek a doctoral degree in clinical or counseling psychology, followed by a predoctoral or postdoctoral internship (i.e., field experience) in forensic psychology, specializing in forensic assessments, and licensure (see Chapter 8 for more information about graduate training and licensure). At the time of this writing, a number of doctoral-level forensic psychology programs are emerging. If you consider applying to a forensic psychology program instead of a clinical or counseling psychology program, be sure that the program is accredited by the American Psychological Association (a quality-check stamp of approval) and meets your state's requirements for licensure.

Seek to develop a solid understanding of pathology, clinical assessment, and treatment, experience with both criminal and noncriminal clients, and an understanding of social and cultural norms and issues. You'll need to understand theory and scientific methodology (e.g., knowledge of scientific validity issues, research design, statistics, and testing) in order to explain the validity of your assessments in a written report or oral presentation. Also consider taking a few courses in law to gain opportunities to read legal cases and observe legal proceedings, which will help to familiarize you with the legal aspects of forensic psychology.

POLICE PSYCHOLOGY

Police psychology has become increasingly prominent in law enforcement (Delprino & Bahn, 1988) despite the wariness that some law enforcement officers hold regarding psychological services (Max, 2000). Police psychologists may be independently practicing consultants to law enforcement agencies or may be employed by law enforcement agencies (sometimes sworn in as law enforcement officers; Bartol, 1996).

Activities of Police Psychologists

Police psychologists provide a variety of evaluative, counseling, training and support services to police agencies, including the following (Scrivner & Kurke, 1995):

- **Selection of Police Officers** One of the most common activities of police psychologists is to provide preemployment evaluations (Super, 1999). Police work is very stressful and requires individuals who are psychologically healthy and prepared for the many challenges entailed in law enforcement. Police psychologists evaluate applicants to rule out those who lack the disposition and personality style to cope with the stress that goes along with a law enforcement career.

- **Training of Police Officers** Police psychologists train officers to enhance their human relations skills including how to be sensitive to victims' needs and understand the nature of, and make appropriates response to, domestic violence. Other areas of psychological training that police psychologists provide include hostage negotiation, policies for reducing police brutality, and strategies for dealing with terrorists.

- **Fitness for Duty and Special Unit Evaluations** Critical incidents, such as death of a partner or injury in the line of duty, can cause tremendous stress. Police psychologists evaluate officers who have been exposed to critical incidents to determine their ability to cope and return to duty. Police psychologists also conduct assessments to assist with promotional decisions for specialized police assignments such as Special Weapons and Tactics (SWAT) or Hostage Negotiation Teams (HNT).

- **Counseling** Stress is a prevalent problem in law enforcement (Anson & Bloom, 1988). Police psychologists provide counseling services to help officers and their families cope with the stressful lifestyle a career in law enforcement entails.

- **Operational Support** Police psychologists provide officers with field consultation (e.g., assisting in the apprehension or security of a mentally ill person, or determining whether a death occurred by homicide or suicide), hostage negotiations and, less frequently, investigative activities (Bartol, 1996). They also communicate the relevant current research literature (e.g., influences on the accuracy of eyewitnesses or identification through police lineups, and how interrogative suggestibility may influence a suspect) to police in order to increase the effectiveness of investigations.

- **Organizational Development and Support** Police psychologists assist management with administrative decision making, team building, and organizational development.

Police psychology encompasses a broad range of activities, but not all police psychologists engage in each of these activities. Police psychologists tend to spend most of their time in counseling, and screening and selection of law enforcement officers (Bartol, 1996; Bergen, Aceto, & Chadziewicz, 1992).

Advantages and Disadvantages to a Career in Police Psychology

A career in police psychology offers opportunities to help law enforcement officers deal with the stresses of their jobs, and to help the community at large. Although some police psychologists might experience mistrust on the part of officers (Wrightsman, 2001), research suggests that most police psychologists perceive little animosity from officers (Bergen et al., 1992).

Perhaps the largest disadvantage to this career is stress. Police departments are very busy and demanding places. Often police psychologists are asked to help with a variety of tasks, which is exciting and interesting, but also taxing. Many police psychologist feel as if they are asked to be all things to all people and sometimes are asked to work in areas that are beyond their expertise or competence (Super, 1999). Needless to say, balancing multiple duties can be draining; the high levels of stress that police psychologists experience can lead to burn out.

Although it is a demanding profession, police psychologists report very high levels of job satisfaction (Bergen et al., 1992). Entry-level salaries for police psychologists are commensurate with other entry-level doctoral psychology positions, with an average entry level annual salary in the $40,000–50,000 range (Kuther & Morgan, 2004). Finally, police psychology is a growth field. Surveys of police psychologists show that they perceive the current and future job market as very good, with excellent opportunities for expansion (Bartol, 1996).

Preparation for a Career in Police Psychology

Most police psychologists are trained as clinical or counseling psychologists. There are very few formal opportunities for training in police psychology during graduate school. If you're interested in a career as a police psychologist, develop excellent clinical skills in assessment, diagnosis, treatment, and crisis intervention (Bartol, 1996). Supplement your clinical and counseling knowledge with courses in psychology and law to understand the legal issues that influence clinical practice within the criminal justice system. An understanding of job analysis procedures, team building, and leadership from courses in industrial and organizational psychology will serve you well (Bartol, 1996). A background in statistics and research methodology will round out your background and provide you with the necessary expertise to evaluate programs and initiatives within police departments. Finally, seek predoctoral and postdoctoral internship or practica experience in police or criminal justice settings in order to obtain practical (and very valuable) experience in police psychology.

RECOMMENDED READINGS

Arrigo, B. A. (2000). *Introduction to Forensic Psychology: Issues and Controversies in Crime and Justice.* San Diego, CA: Academic Press.

Bartol, C. R. (1996). Police psychology then, now, and beyond. Criminal Justice and Behavior, 23, 70–89.

Blau, T. H. (1994). Psychological services for law enforcement. New York: Wiley.

Kurke, M. I., & Scrivner, E. M. (1995). *Police psychology into the 21st century.* Hillsdale, NJ: Erlbaum.

Hess, A. K., & Weiner, I. B. (1999). *The handbook of forensic psychology.* New York: Wiley.

Huss, M. T. (2001). What is forensic psychology ? It's not *Silence of the Lambs! Eye of Psi Chi,* 5(3), 25–27. (available at http://www.psichi.org/content/publications/eye/volume/vol_5/5_3/huss.asp)

Wrightsman, L. S. (2001). *Forensic psychology.* Belmont, CA: Wadsworth.

WEB RESOURCES

American Board of Forensic Psychology
http://www.abfp.com/

American Psychology-Law Society
http://www.unl.edu/ap-ls/

David Willshire's Forensic Psychology & Psychiatry Links
http://members.optushome.com.au/dwillsh/

Careers in Forensic Psychology
http://www.wcupa.edu/_ACADEMICS/sch_cas.psy/Career_Paths/Forensic/Career08.htm

Forensic Psychology
http://faculty.ncwc.edu/toconnor/425/425lect18.htm

Forensic Psychology Services
http://www.psychologyinfo.com/forensic/

Heavy Badge
http://www.heavybadge.com/

International Association of Chiefs of Police
http://www.theiacp.org/div_sec_com/sections/Psych_Srvcs/fitness.htm

National Criminal Justice Reference Service
http://www.ncjrs.org/

Police Psychology Online
http://www.policepsych.com/

The Society for Police and Criminal Psychology
http://cep.jmu.edu/spcp/

PROFILE 5.1: KAREN FRANKLIN, PH.D.

Karen Franklin, Ph.D., earned her doctorate in clinical psychology at the California School of Professional Psychology. She is licensed in the states of California and Washington, and has completed a postdoctoral fellowship in forensic psychology at the University of Washington. She is a widely recognized expert on the psychosocial motivations of hate-crime offenders. Her research on this topic has garnered the Monette/Horwitz Trust Award (2001) and Harry Frank Guggenheim Fellowship (1996). Her peer-reviewed publications have appeared in *American Behavioral Scientist, Journal of Interpersonal Violence, Encyclopedia of Violence, Encyclopedia of Criminology*, and *Journal of Forensic Psychology Practice*, among others. Currently, she has an independent forensic practice in the San Francisco Bay Area, specializing in the evaluation of adult offenders. She also teaches forensic psychology at the California School of Professional Psychology. Dr. Franklin explains how she became interested in forensic psychology and what her job entails.

Forensic psychology is not my first career, nor even my second. I previously worked as a typesetter, a newspaper reporter, a private investigator, and even a tobacco barner. Of all of my careers, forensic psychology is the ideal one for someone with a low threshold for boredom.

I became interested in forensic psychology while working as a criminal investigator. I was putting together "mitigating evidence" for defendants facing capital murder trials. Working on a team with experts and attorneys, I observed that forensic psychologists got paid good money to do what I liked best—studying what makes people tick.

My undergraduate education in journalism and my career as an investigator armed me with two tools essential to the forensic psychologist—writing skills and detective skills. After obtaining a Ph.D. in clinical psychology, I pursued advanced training in forensic psychology through a postdoctoral fellowship. To further hone my skills in preparation for independent practice, I also worked briefly at two prisons and a mental hospital.

My forensic practice focuses on adult criminal cases. In a typical week, I might conduct evaluations at several jails, consult with attorneys, review research on various topics, and write reports of my findings. The issues I tackle are varied. The bread-and-butter work is evaluating defendants' competency to stand trial. Other frequent issues include a defendant's mental state at the time of an offense or a person's risk of future violence or sexual offending. At other times, I am involved as a "pure expert," that is, someone who discusses the empirical literature on a topic without evaluating any of the parties in a case.

Like many forensic psychologists, I stay active in academic and research pursuits as well. I teach forensic psychology to graduate students, review articles for publication in journals, and occasionally write an article in my research area. Fortuitously, my dissertation topic—the motivations of hate-crime offenders—garnered a lot of interest at the time, and I earned some prominence in that niche. This has some overlay with my clinical practice, in that I may be called on to evaluate a defendant if anti-gay bias is a suspected element.

As compared with general clinical psychology, forensic work has distinct advantages and disadvantages. On the plus side, the work is fascinating, and it provides enormous variety. I have a great deal of independence, and some ability to pick and choose the work. Forensic psychologists are also accorded quite a bit of respect in the legal arena.

At the same time, the work is hard, and requires rigorous attention to detail. The practitioner must stay up to date on the latest developments in numerous areas. She must be skilled at psychological testing. Under adversarial scrutiny, a mistake can be costly, leading to public embarrassment or worse. Excellent writing skills are essential, as we write numerous and lengthy reports and our written presentation can make or break our reputation. Forensic psychologists must also develop the business acumen and thick skin necessary to deal with attorneys and other clients who may have agendas that conflict with our values, ethics, or practical interests.

At the present time, there is no single acceptable training model for forensic psychologists. Students interested in pursuing a career in forensic psychology should get a firm undergraduate and graduate foundation in the science of psychology (including issues of research design, statistics, and testing). Then, select one or more career niches, and take courses relevant to these. For example, if you intend to do child custody work, you should become an expert on child development. If you intend to work with juvenile offenders, pursue an internship in an adolescent setting. Become especially knowledgeable about cultural and social influences on behavior. Some course work on legal theory is also advantageous. The dissertation has a potential to open doors, so the topic should be carefully chosen. It should be something that not only fascinates you, but also has potential marketability. (Hint: Do _not_ study the mind of the serial killer!)

After obtaining a doctoral degree in clinical psychology, I recommend pursuing a formal postgraduate fellowship through which you can get the advanced training, experience, and mentoring necessary to launch a successful career. Ideally, this should be in the geographic locale and among the population with whom you intend to work. I also recommend working in a forensic hospital or correctional setting during your training or early career. Stay in these settings only long enough to become familiar with their workings, and not so long that your values become corrupted by them.

(Reprinted with permission from Kuther, 2004.)

PROFILE 5.2: EVAN NELSON

Dr. Evan Nelson is a Licensed Clinical Psychologist and a Certified Sex Offender Treatment Provider in the Commonwealth of Virginia. He holds a Diplomate in Forensic Psychology from the American Board of Professional Psychology (ABPP). He earned his Ph.D. in clinical psychology from the University of North Carolina at Chapel Hill, completed an internship at the Indiana University School of Medicine, and performed his postdoctoral residency at the Forensic Unit of Central State Hospital in Petersburg, Virginia. Dr. Nelson has been an expert in thousands of criminal cases including more than 150 capital murder trials, and his work has been cited in 18 Virginia Appellate and Supreme Court decisions as well as the recent U.S. Supreme Court decision on *Atkins* v. *Commonwealth*.

Dr. Nelson provided responses to several questions I posed concerning his background and assessment of the field of forensic psychology.

How did you become interested in forensic psychology?

The fact that my career is in forensic psychology had more to do with opportunity knocking than with any preplanning. In graduate school, I trained as a generalist in clinical psychology, with the hope of practicing marital and family therapy as a specialty. However, after my internship I needed to get a job in Richmond, Virginia, because that was where my wife's psychology internship was going to be—and a position at Virginia's flagship forensic inpatient was the best employment I could find at the time. There were no good positions in marital and family therapy for an entry-level doctor when I needed a job, and hence I became a forensic specialist.

In retrospect I consider myself lucky that I fell into the forensic hospital job. It turned out that I liked working with patients with more severe psychopathology, enjoyed the detective-like work of conducting a forensic evaluation, and loved the intense experience of testifying at a trial. Seeing a crime through the eyes of a mentally ill defendant is an extraordinary way to come to understand the power of the mind and its influence on behavior. Working in a forensic hospital provided in-depth training and a wealth of professional contacts that made it easy to transition to private practice after three years of experience.

What are your specialties and areas of expertise?

The bulk of my practice is evaluations of criminal defendants to see if they are competent to stand trial, legally insane at the time of the alleged offense, and to assess issues related to sentencing. I have special expertise in the areas of capital sentencing (death penalty hearings) and sex offender risk assessment. In addition to criminal evaluations, I also evaluate persons applying for disability and fathers engaged in custody battles who have been accused of sexual improprieties.

A typical day involves traveling to a jail or prison, interviewing and testing a defendant, reviewing the offense and treatment records related to the case, contacting witnesses to the crime or family members of the defendant to learn their perspectives on what happened and the defendant's mental health history, consulting with the lawyers, and then writing a report. In about 1 of 20 cases, I testify about my results.

What trends do you see for forensic psychology?

It is my opinion that forensic psychology will grow while many other sectors of psychology will shrink. The world is becoming more litigious, society is becoming more conservative and therefore prosecuting more cases, and the failing economy after 9/11/01 will mean a rise in crime over the next few years—all of which creates opportunities for forensic specialists. The high visibility of forensic psychology via Court TV, television shows such as *CSI* and *Profiler*, and criminal cases of national interest (e.g., Andrea Yates's insanity plea in Texas, questions about the competency of Zacarias Moussaoui to plead guilty to conspiracy in the World Trade Center bombing) has already led to increased interest in the field.

In addition, the psycholegal arena is one of the few domains left where a doctorate degree is a requisite credential and where persons with advanced degrees are compensated for their special expertise. I predict that psychologists in general clinical practice will increasingly diversify their practices to include forensics because they can be paid well and have professional prestige; I never have to haggle with an insurance company, as do mainstream therapists.

The field of forensic psychology is also likely to become more data focused. In the past 10 years, the complexity of psychological tests has increased and the legal system is demanding that experts provide more proof for the validity of their procedures (see *Daubert* v. *Merrill Dow Pharmaceuticals*). With the advent of high-speed Internet connections, some aspects of forensic psychology will probably transition to videotelephone consultations, somewhat like telemedicine.

What advantages/disadvantages do you see to becoming a forensic psychologist?

As noted above, in my opinion there is more job security in forensics than in being a general therapist because of the economics of the changing marketplace for psychology. On average, forensic psychologists earn more money than their counterparts whose practices focus on non-forensic therapy. The work itself is very exciting in large part because of the nature of criminal cases, but also because being an expert means one is an important part of the legal process and in a unique position to educate lawyers, judges, and juries about mental health and mental illness.

On the other hand, this is a stressful business. The successful forensic expert needs a veneer of cynicism and a thick skin to survive. This field involves working closely with criminals who have done heinous deeds, coping with the raw emotions of victims as well as the family members of the defendants, and even life-and-death matters such as in a death penalty hearing. One has to be able to stay emotionally detached from the details of the case. Being an expert can be bruising on the ego, too: testimony can be brutal and attorneys and the media often comment on an expert's credibility or personality without any opportunity for the psychologist to respond.

The pace of the job is very rapid: courts and lawyers demand a rapid response from experts, even though legal proceedings themselves make take months or years to reach a conclusion. Thus, being able to tolerate stress and constant change are critical elements in the practice of forensic. Frequently, forensic experts must travel to perform evaluations outside of their vicinity and this can be a strain on family life.

(Reprinted with permission from Kuther, 2004.)

PROFILE 5.3: ELLEN KIRCHMAN, PH.D.

Ellen Kirschman, Ph.D., is an atypical police psychologist. She doesn't work for a specific department or practice; she works for herself. And, she doesn't do many officer screenings.

Her practice focuses on providing police officer crisis interventions, police department management consultations, seminars for law enforcement and public outreach, as well as conducting some research. "I'm sort of like a cop myself [in that] I like to have a lot of variety in my work life," says Kirschman.

She spends one day a week at the Palo Alto, Calif., Police Department as the health resources coordinator, talking to officers and civilian employees after stressful incidents, helping them find mental health services for themselves and their families, consulting with managers and supervisors, and assisting recruits and field training officers.

"My office is right there on the flight path between the briefing room and the locker room, as opposed to being tucked away," she says. "It ensures that I'm part of the general mix of the whole organization."

Kirschman is also part of a team of psychologists helping another local public safety department start a peer-support team to assist police officers and firefighters after stressful incidents. She also provides critical incident training and legal and management consultation to several other police and fire departments.

But Kirschman's work isn't limited to her scheduled office hours: Since police work 24 hours a day, 7 days a week, psychologists must be available "24-7" too, she explains.

In addition to consulting with police departments, Kirschman is the author of a widely distributed book for police families, *I Love a Cop: What Police Families Need to Know,* and is co-founder and co-project director of the Web site policefamilies.com. She and fellow police psychologist Lorraine Greene, Ph.D., developed the site to give families of police officers mental health information and access to online family support services.

Funded by the National Institute of Justice, the Metropolitan Police Department of Nashville, Tenn., and Davidson County, Tenn., the site includes message boards and curriculum outlines with downloadable overheads and handouts for educational workshops for spouses, parents and children. Families can also find tips on money management, information on bouncing back from a stressful event and how to be a better communicator, columns written by police psychologists, and a special section for kids.

For several years, she has helped train Drug Enforcement Agency (DEA) agents to provide support to peers and their families after a trauma. Sometimes, she explains, law enforcement personnel react better to support from a colleague than a mental health worker from the outside. In the same vein, she's helped train family members of DEA agents killed in the line of duty to reach out to newly bereaved families.

Kirschman also travels across the country to speak to police officers, police academy students and law enforcement families about coping with job and family stress, as well as to mental health professionals working with police or who are interested in the field.

"My view is that I am working with healthy people who have difficult jobs and a lot of job stress—as opposed to working with a sick population," she says, adding that "you have to keep in mind that these people have been thoroughly screened before they get their jobs; we psychologists never get screened."

(reprinted with permission from Smith, 2002)

Profile 5.4: Gary Kaufmann, Psy.D.

Gary Kaufmann, Psy.D., and his fellow Michigan State Police psychologists operate in two distinct modes: a clinical one, in which they help police officers cope with job stress and mental health issues, and a criminal one in which they help officers track down and arrest criminals.

In their clinical mode, Kaufmann, head of the Michigan State Police's Office of Behavioral Science, and his staff counsel officers who seek assistance for such problems as substance abuse, job stress and family conflicts.

"The department has, from its inception, had a very forward-thinking attitude about mental health services and how they fold into law enforcement," says Kaufmann. "It takes the best advantage of psychologists of any police department in the country. They literally use us to our capacity."

He and his colleagues also respond to critical incidents—such as when an officer is killed in the line of duty or is suicidal—by providing on-the-scene support and follow-up with the affected individuals. And since it can take 16 hours to drive from one corner of Michigan to the other, the police department has no reservations about sending a psychologist to the scene via helicopter, plane or even a rare "red-light relay," where the psychologist hitches a ride from police car to police car—lights flashing and sirens wailing—until he or she reaches the jurisdiction in need of services.

In the criminal mode, Kaufmann's office assists officers in solving crimes and responds to high-pressure situations. "Our job is to help the officer translate the psychological dynamics observed into operational tactics," he says, emphasizing that this kind of work is always a team effort.

For example, a few years ago Kaufmann worked with Michigan State Police detectives to solve the murder of a local television news anchor in Marshall, Mich. At first, investigators believed a stalker or crazed fan shot the woman in her driveway. But after re-examining the way the woman was shot—in the manner of an execution, without any close interaction between the killer and the newscaster—it didn't seem as though a stranger had committed the crime, Kaufmann says. He and his colleagues began focusing on the woman's husband, who was eventually convicted of the murder. The theory the investigative team developed, says Kaufmann, was that the husband was jealous of the attention his wife gave their two children and her career.

"This is an arena in which a different kind of methodology is necessary in order to accomplish the goals of law enforcement: catching the bad guys," he explains. "While, at one end in our clinical work, we uphold the standards of a clinical psychologist to the nth degree, on the other end, those ethical standards just don't apply."

That may mean making judgments about a suspect without ever having direct contact with the person or recommending how to make a suspect more anxious to get a confession—methodologies that Kaufmann says aren't consistent with the typical clinical psychology model.

It's also important, Kaufmann adds, for his staff to understand that while psychologists see the complexities of human behavior, police want definite answers. For example, every time a SWAT team is called into a situation- a weekly occurrence—Kaufmann's office sends a psychologist to the scene. During such a hostage situation, officers may ask Kaufmann if he thinks the suspect will really hurt a hostage. In other words, can the suspect be talked down, or should officers storm the building to rescue those held captive?

"This is one situation where you really need to be able to step up to the plate and make a decision, recognizing that the recommendations you make may have life-or-death consequences," Kaufmann says.

(reprinted with permission from Smith, 2002)

CONSULTING CAREERS

CHAPTER GUIDE

MANAGEMENT CONSULTANT

ADVANTAGES AND DISADVANTAGES
OF A CAREER AS A MANAGEMENT
CONSULTANT

PREPARATION FOR A CAREER AS A
MANAGEMENT CONSULTANT

EXECUTIVE COACH

**ACTIVITIES AND PROFESSIONAL
RESPONSIBILITIES. WHAT DO
EXECUTIVE COACHES DO?**

ADVANTAGES AND DISADVANTAGES
TO A CAREER AS AN EXECUTIVE
COACH

PREPARATION FOR A CAREER AS
AN EXECUTIVE COACH

RECOMMENDED READINGS

WEB RESOURCES

**PROFILE 6.1: STEVEN
WILLIAMS, PH.D., S.P.H.R.**

**PROFILE 6.2: MORE
PSYCHOLOGISTS ARE
ATTRACTED TO THE EXECUTIVE
COACHING FIELD**

Consultants are professionals who help others solve problems in business, research, industry, and government settings. There are many different kinds of consultants. In this chapter we'll examine two consulting careers that psychologists in clinical and counseling psychology sometimes enter: management consulting and executive coaching.

MANAGEMENT CONSULTANT

Management consulting is a broad term for many consulting careers. Management consultants solve business problems by applying hypothesis testing and data analysis techniques. Because business leaders and managers handle many concerns, they turn to management consultants for assistance with a variety of issues. Consultants often specialize in specific management concerns. Consider the following types of management consultants:

- Strategic management consultants advise companies on business strategy, such as how to grow a business; what operations to perform; whether to enter new geographic markets, launch new products, buy other businesses, and so on.
- Operations management consultants study how to improve operational efficiency, including how to reduce waste and improve productivity.
- Information technology consultants advise organizations about technology issues, such as whether their accounting software meets their needs, how to manage the vast amounts of information needed to operate the business, and how to create and organize databases for maximum efficiency and security.
- Executive search consultants are high-level recruiters, often called "headhunters," who use their knowledge of industrial and organizational psychology to recruit, assess, and place employees in top positions.
- Organizational development consultants help companies with team building, training (e.g., teaching communication and conflict management skills), dealing with change, and professional development.

Generally, then, management consultants work with clients to help them develop and implement strategies for creating and sustaining successful businesses. They work with other consultants or company employees to analyze a problem and brainstorm potential solutions. Management consultants develop initial hypotheses and test them through logical analysis and research. Articles, observations, surveys, and interviews are collected and analyzed to draw conclusions. Then consultants communicate findings and recommendations to clients and assist with implementing and monitoring solutions.

Advantages and Disadvantages of a Career as a Management Consultant

A primary advantage of a career in management consulting is that you'll always be encouraged to learn new things. Every project brings new challenges and opportunities. Many management consultants explain that there is a steep learning curve because each project requires learning about a new field and new company. You'll meet and work with many different people of diverse backgrounds, training, and interests. The people part of management consulting—communicating with others and solving interpersonal problems—can be stimulating, but also exhausting, especially because there's no predicting how a company's employees will react to your presence. Some will embrace you and your efforts to help them improve; others may be wary and unhelpful. Even entry-level management consultants are given much responsibility as well as exposure to a company's senior executives. Your suggestions are heard and can make a big difference. Alternatively, the responsibility can be overwhelming as you'll be held accountable for errors and misjudgment.

Management consulting usually entails a great deal of travel. You'll travel to where your clients are located, sometimes spending weeks conducting research or implementing solutions on the road. Business travel can be glamorous, but it can also strain relationships with family and friends. Management consulting is hard work requiring creativity and dedication. Long hours (55–70 per week) are common and the overall pace of work is fast.

The travel, long hours, and stress of a career in management consulting are matched by high salaries. The median income for all consultants is $64,793). Among doctoral-level industrial/organizational psychologist consultants, the median salary in 2001 was $92,500 (Singleton, Tate, & Randall, 2003). Though consulting is a competitive field, it's expected to grow faster than the average for all occupations through 2010 (Bureau of Labor Statistics, 2002).

Preparing for a Career as a Management Consultant

Psychology graduates are well suited to careers in consulting because they have advanced analytical skills. Develop your ability to analyze data, use statistics, manage databases (such as SPSS, Microsoft Access, and others), and present data simply and elegantly through the use of tables and graphs. Develop communication by taking additional courses in writing and public speaking. Your understanding of psychological theories and "how people work" are assets, but you need to be able to apply your understanding and explain it to businesspeople in ways that they can understand and appreciate. Because teamwork is an essential part of the job of management consultant, an understanding of interpersonal skills, group dynamics, and leadership will come in handy; take courses in these areas, in social psychology, and consider a minor or concentration in business administration.

Finally, be prepared to sell your degree, specifically the skills that graduate students in psychology acquire (such as methodological, statistical, interpersonal, and problem-solving skills), as employers may not be familiar with psychology. Communicate your strengths to potential employers. Make contacts, get experience, and meet potential employers by completing an internship with a management consulting firm.

EXECUTIVE COACH

An executive coach is a consultant who focuses on helping professionals to maximize their fulfillment in work by equipping them with the "tools, knowledge, and opportunities they need to develop themselves and become more effective" (Peterson & Hicks, 1996). Executive coaching is similar to management consulting in that the goal is to improve professional functioning; however, the emphasis is on the individual executive as opposed to the organization at large (Garman, Whiston, & Zlatoper, 2000). Executive coaches work one-on-one with executives and focus on making leaders more effective by helping them to identity their strengths and weaknesses, address them, and enhance leadership and management skills (Kilburg, 1996; Witherspoon & White, 1996). An executive coach might assist a manager who has never supervised before, serve as a sounding board for strategic decision making, or help a professional cope with stress (Foxhall, 2002). Executive coaching is intended to bring out the best in people. As Witherspoon and White (1996) explain, "The word *coach*, first used in English in the 1500s, refers to a particular kind of carriage… Hence, the root meaning of the verb 'to coach' is to convey a valued person from one was to where one wants to be—a solid meaning for coaching executives today" (p. 124).

ACTIVITIES AND PROFESSIONAL RESPONSIBILITIES. WHAT DO EXECUTIVE COACHES DO?

The task of executive coaches is one of facilitation more so than teaching. Coaches help their clients learn as well as make the most of their learning. Coaches may embody several roles (Whiterspoon & White, 1996):

- Skill-based coaching, which focuses on helping a client learn skills needed for a specific task (e.g., conducting job interviews).
- Performance-based coaching, which focuses on helping a client improve his or her job-related performance by learning new strategies, methods, behaviors, attitudes, and perspectives that are associated with success.
- Development-based coaching, or helping clients prepare for a future job by learning skills and attitudes needed for advancement.

- Coaching for the executive's agenda, which is coaching designed to help the executive manage the daily decisions, hassles, and stresses of professional life (e.g., helping the client make progress on self-identified goals, being a sounding board for the client to share ideas and strategies)

Coaching is an ongoing confidential relationship with client oriented toward producing change. The coach takes a prospective orientation, helping the client to identify goals and maximize potential to achieve fulfillment in life and work (Hart, Blattner, & Leipsic, 2001). Clinical and counseling psychologists' therapeutic and counseling skills are useful in careers as executive coaches; however, executive coaching is not therapy or counseling. The ultimate goal of coaching is to improve the executive's interpersonal skills and work performance and therefore, it is more issue-focused than therapy (Kampa-Kokesch & Anderson, 2001).

Coaching also occurs in a broader variety of contexts than does therapy, including face-to-face sessions at work, in a coach's office, and at other information locations such as coffee shops, as well as over the telephone and by e-mail (Kampa-Kokesch & Anderson, 2001). The relationship between coach and client differs markedly from that of therapist and client in that it is more collegial, informal, and supportive, with less self-disclosure on the part of the executive (Kampa-Kokesch& Anderson, 2001; Levinson, 1996). Conversations center around work and business objectives—and are active and interactive, with the coach asking questions, providing examples, and suggesting solutions. Coaches who conducted therapy explain that they are more likely to use humor, be more actively engaged, and have greater flexibility in the coaching relationship than in the traditional therapeutic relationship (Hart et al., 2001). The coach's job is to help clients "translate insight into action" (Peterson, 1996, p. 85) by probing what they've learned as well as what they will do and how will they use what they've learned. The goal of coaching is to teach clients to help themselves develop.

Advantages and Disadvantages to a Career as an Executive Coach

A career as an executive coach offers constant change, challenges, and independence. Coaching is conducted in person and by phone, so there's a tremendous amount of flexibility. Many executive coaches have independent practices, and some are employed as internal coaches for organizations or for consulting firms. If you seek an independent practice, expect to spend significant resources and time on marketing and developing a client base (review the challenges of independent practice, as discussed in Chapter 2). Once established, a career as an independently practicing executive coach is lucrative. Most executive coaches charge between $200 and $500 per hour (Grodzki, 2002). Executive coaches who join consulting firms also earn comfortable salaries, as we've seen.

A critical challenge to the executive coaching field is it's lack of regulation (Hart et al., 2001). There is no universally accepted certification for executive coaching; nor are there standard definitions of coaching or regulations governing good practice (Garman et al., 2000). However, coaching is likely to become regulated in the coming years (Hart et al., 2001). For example, many executive coaches in the state of Washington interpret the definition of counselor, a regulated label, to include coaching:

> (5) 'Counseling" means employing any therapeutic techniques, including but not limited to social work, mental health counseling, marriage and family therapy, and hypnotherapy, for a fee that offer, assist or attempt to assist an individual or individuals in the amelioration or adjustment of mental, emotional or behavioral problems, and includes therapeutic techniques to achieve sensitivity and awareness of the self and others and the development of human potential (Revised Code of Washington, 1987, as cited in Hart et al., 2001).

Many coaches in Washington state have sought certification because counselors as the coach's emphasis on becoming aware of one's abilities and potential—and on actualizing potential—may fall under this definition of counseling. We are likely to see many more changes in this area, so it's essential that you remain aware of this issue if you intend to practice as an executive coach.

Similarly, executive coaching entails self-monitoring challenges. Because coaching is an umbrella term similar to management consulting, it's important for psychologists who coach to remain vigilant in assessing their own competence and communicate with clients regarding exactly what types of problems they are qualified to work on (Foxhall, 2002). Executive coaching requires a different, complementary set of skills than those that the clinical and counseling psychologist develops (Sommerville, 1998). Psychologists must be aware of their level of competence and work to obtain needed skills to improve their ability to assist executives. Despite these challenges to developing a career as an executive coach, psychologists who seek innovative applied opportunities outside of the realm of managed care should consider a career in executive coaching, because it receives lots of media attention and is a growing career field (Garman, et al., 2000).

PREPARATION FOR A CAREER AS AN EXECUTIVE COACH

If you're interested in becoming an executive coach, recognize that training in clinical or counseling psychology must be supplemented with a comprehensive background in industrial and organizational psychology. Applied experience in the business world and an understanding of leadership and management in organizational settings will enhance your preparation for a career as an executive coach. In other words, becoming an executive coach requires eclectic training.

Psychologists who are trained in industrial or organizational psychology must learn more about clinical and developmental issues that can influence a leader's effectiveness (and vice versa for those trained in clinical or counseling psychology). That said, clinical and counseling psychologists have a special advantage in working with executives because their training in normative and pathological functioning enables them to identify when a coaching client is in need of referral, unlike coaches who are not clinicians.

An interest in business and understanding of the demands of leadership roles is essential (Foxhall, 2002), so seek internships in business settings and seek apprenticeship relationships with experienced executive coaches (Glasser, 2002). Executive coaches help managers and leaders develop interpersonal skills, therefore excellent interpersonal and relational skills are essential. Also seek to develop skills in active listening, objective setting, creating action plans, and evaluating implementation plans and interventions (Glasser, 2002). A career as an executive coach requires broad generalist skills, so seek a range of applied experiences and coursework in industrial and organizational psychology, social psychology, business, management, and adult development.

RECOMMENDED READINGS

Aamodt, M. G. (2003). *Applied industrial/organizational psychology.* Pacific Grove, CA: Wadsworth.

Fitzgerald, C., & Berger, J. G. (Eds). (2002). *Executive coaching: Practices & perspectives.* Palo Alto, CA: Davies-Black.

Kilburg, R. R. (1996). Toward a conceptual understanding and definition of executive coaching. *Consulting Psychology Journal: Practice and Research, 48,* 134–144.

Naifcy, M. (1997). *The fast track: The insider's guide to winning jobs in management consulting, investment banking, and securities trading.* New York: Broadway Books.

Peltier, B. (2001). *The psychology of executive coaching: Theory and application.* Philadelphia: Taylor & Francis.

Schwartz, N. (1995). An interesting career in psychology: Executive search consultant. *Psychological Science Agenda.* Retrieved on May 23, 2003, at http://www.apa.org/science/ic-schwartz.html

Smith, P. M. (1997). An interesting career in psychology: Organizational development consultant. *Psychological Science Agenda.* Retrieved on May 23, 2003, at http://www.apa.org/science/ic-smith.html

Stout, C. E., & Fairley, S. (2003). Getting started in personal and executive coaching : How to create a thriving coaching practice. Hoboken, NJ: Wiley.

WEB RESOURCES

Academy of Management
  http://www.aomonline.org/

Careers in Consulting
  http://www.careers-in-business.com/consulting/mc.htm

The Center for the Study of Work Teams
  http://www.workteams.unt.edu/

Society for Industrial and Organizational Psychology
  http://siop.org/

Professional Industrial Organizational Psychologist Network
  http://www.piop.net

Society for Human Resource Management
  http://www.shrm.org/

Society of Consulting Psychology
  http://www.apa.org/divisions/div13/

The Value of an Executive Coach
  http://change.monster.com/articles/execcoach/

PROFILE 6.1: STEVEN WILLIAMS, PH.D., S.P.H.R.

Steve Williams, Ph.D., is the Director of Research at the Society for Human Resource Management. He was trained as a clinical psychologist and is currently licensed, but has spent most of his professional career dealing with workplace, personnel, and organizational issues. He has written several publications on these topics, and has conducted workshops for various types of executives. I asked Dr. Williams several questions about his background and work with executives.

Describe your background. How did you become interested in psychology?

My original interest was in psychiatry. Fortunately, I took advantage of several volunteer opportunities as an undergraduate that gave me a preview of the type of career that I intended to pursue. For example, I volunteered in psychiatric units of hospitals, community psychiatric clinics, and residential psychiatric treatment centers. As a result, I was able to to get exposure to various types of profesionals such as psychiatrists, clinical psychologists, social workers, and the like. I quickly learned that psychiatry was not for me due to the very narrow medical model that became the solution to most or all problems. I gained a deeper respect for clinical psychologists, who seemed to take a multifaceted approach and gain a deeper understanding of the problem at hand.When it came time to apply to graduate programs in clinical psychology, I only focused on those programs that prescribed to the so-called Boulder model—an equal balance between clinical and research training. The diversity of skills offered by my graduate program became the foundation of my career and the springboard that allowed me to approach my career in a very nontraditional manner.

What are your particular areas of expertise or interest?

The two areas that have become specialty areas for me are applied organizational research and consulting. Both of these areas involve almost all of the skills that I learned in my clinical psychology graduate program. Applying organizational research involves expertise in developing benchmarking instruments, statistical sampling, data collection (via mail, Internet, telephone, or other means), data analysis, report writing and debriefing. It also involves doing these tasks quickly and efficiently. One particularly needs to have a knack for asking the right type of questions based on the issues the organization is facing. On the consulting side, it involves helping executives use benchmarking statistics to make important decisions. It is important to be able to translate technical terms into very simple layperson's language. This area taps into the clinical side to my training, as it involves intense listening, use of persuasion, diagnosing or conceptualizing problems within the organization, and devising solutions. For example, the skills that underlie psychodiagnostic interviewing and psychotherapy are very similar to the skills necessary to help executives diagnose workplace issues and dynamics, manage their subordinates, increase workplace motivation, and produce change in the workplace. Oftentimes, management issues are people issues. As remarkable as it may sound, I have discovered that learning how to manage people can actually have an impact on the organization's bottom line.

Describe your employment setting and the activities in which you engage. How do you spend your days?

Perhaps the best way to describe how I spend my professional time is by helping executives (e.g., human resource professionals, CFOs, CEOs, and other executives) use research to make management decisions. I oversee a large research department that conducts research on various topics in management and human resources, and then helps professionals use this research in their daily roles. For example, we may help an HR professional use research to convince her CEO that increasing the headcount in the organization is likely to considerably increase the organization's revenue. Or we may provide the CEO with empirical data that shows investing in training employees provides a favorable impact on the bottom line.

An example: I was recently asked by a chief executive officer (CEO) of a Washington DC company for a compensation and contract analysis. More often than not, a company or its board of directors requests and pays for compensation and contract analyses. However, the unique circumstances faced by this CEO prompted her to contact me directly. The CEO believed that she was considerably underpaid for someone of her years of experience and background, and that the benefits and "perks" that were in her contract also were not commensurate with that of hr peers. Because her contract was up for renewal, she thought this was an ideal opportunity to negotiate a better package.

Based on CEO compensation data that I previously collected from almost 1,000 CEOs, I was able to extensively examine compensation, benefits, and terms of contracts for those CEOs whose organizations matched her organization's revenue size, staff type, company type, industry and focus. I was able to match her against peers with similar years of experience, degree level, and other credentials. After careful analysis, the benchmarking data suggested that she was indeed paid considerably less than her peers. The hard data were used as a negotiating tool, and her board of directors eventually agreed to a more competitive compensation package than she was previously awarded.

What are the advantages and disadvantages of your career choice and setting? What should students know in considering such a career?

One advantage to my career choice is that it is an expanding field, and executives are increasingly relying on the skills and expertise of those who can tell them how to run their organizations best. There are a multitude of opportunities and workplace settings, and this is likely to increase in the near future. Another advantage is that it is a financially rewarding career for psychology degree recipients, even for recent graduates in psychology. Within a few years, it is not farfetched for recent graduates to earn a six-figure salary if one lands in the right setting. Depending on your niche, clientele, and expertise, the salary ceiling is as high as what you can convince someone to pay you for your services and time.

There is a downside. Even though there are a multitude of factors that can determine whether business decisions proceed as planned, if your research or consultation played a large role in a decision that took a wrong turn, you may find yourself blamed or targeted unjustly as the scapegoat. It may even be due to someone not following your advice or someone not interpreting the data correctly. In the business world, someone seemingly looks "pass the buck," especially when highly paid executives are involved. Al in all, however, I do believe the advantages outweigh the disadvantages.

How can students prepare themselves for such a career?

My advice to students is to think about your career ambitions at the earliest possible stages, and also think about what type of job you would like. Too often, psychology students only think about their first job during their final year of training. By that time, they have missed opportunities to take relevant coursework, develop skills, and gain relevant exposure.

At the earliest stages of your training, be open to volunteering part of your time in an applied organizational research setting or management consulting setting (If you are not thinking about management consulting specifically, I still recommend getting exposure in your area of interest by volunteering as early as possible). Volunteering was what caused me to change career directions because it made me "think outside the box." This seems to be an overused cliché but worth repeating because traditionally, psychology students are not trained to "think outside the box" when it comes to making career decisions. Students must avoid being pigeonholed into the typical career paths. This restricted thought pattern only limits your career options. Instead, you should identify the micro-skills inherent in psychology training, and learn how to apply those skills and knowledge in various settings.

PROFILE 6.2: MORE PSYCHOLOGISTS ARE ATTRACTED TO THE EXECUTIVE COACHING FIELD

Psychologists who have ventured into the executive coaching field say there's great opportunity for more of their colleagues to enter the field—if they understand and care about business.

The work, which focuses on making top leaders more effective, has come into its own, says Sandra Shullman, Ph.D., chair of APA's Executive Coaching Work Group, an effort of the Board of Professional Affairs. "Executive coaching is a workplace trend and a trend in psychology," she says.

While Fortune 500 companies have used this kind of consultation for some time, it's becoming increasingly common for smaller entities like family businesses, dentists or attorneys to use the service.

"There is a huge opportunity," says Karol M. Wasylyshyn, Psy.D., who has done the work for about 20 years. "Businesses of all types continue to invest a lot in executive coaching."

WHAT IT IS

In terms of everything executive coaches might do, "the possibilities become mind-boggling," says Randall P. White, Ph.D., principal in the Executive Development Group and co-author of "The Glass Ceiling: Can Women Reach the Top of America's Largest Corporations?" The work often is about helping an executive identify his or her strengths and weaknesses and address both, but other areas of focus many include:

• Serving as a sounding board for strategic decision making.

• Coaching a newly promoted employee who has never supervised before.

• Helping employees manage their stress.

• Helping a team "fight fair" as its members divide up resources for their parts of a make-or-break product development.

• Aiding in the "management of uncertainty" in these days when there can be five or six "right" strategies that could be pursued.

• Mediating conflicts between executives. A coach often has a kind of temporary authority, say several of the experts, to tell top leaders what no one else can. "Sometimes I can say the unsayable," says White.

Far from being a management fad, executive coaching has lasting impetus behind it, say those in the field. "There are talent wars ongoing in industry," says Shullman, and companies increasingly want to retain people by developing them into higher roles or helping them function in current roles.

In addition, Shullman says, globalization, technology and corporate mergers have so stepped up the pace of change that top leaders "don't have all the answers anymore." That means they have to rely on and engage the people they supervise much more than in the past, using the people skills they may not have developed.

Rodney Lowman, Ph.D., who has started a Ph.D. program in consulting psychology at California's Alliant University, says part of the explanation for the "explosive growth" in executive coaching is that it fills some of the same needs as psychotherapy, but it has never had a stigma attached to it. Executive coaching he says, is "about positive things like growth and maximizing potential."

The declining economy and the uneasiness felt in many companies following the Sept. 11 attacks have also advanced the coaching marketplace, adds industrial/organizational (I/O) psychologist Nancy Tippins, Ph.D., who has worked with businesses for 20 years.

"Executives have tough jobs, particularly now with this economy, and it is increasingly difficult to be responsible for lots of people," says Tippins, who is president of Personnel Research Associates in Dallas, a consulting firm that does executive coaching. "Organizations want to invest in those activities that help executives be most productive."

WHAT IT TAKES

Seasoned experts in the field sound a note of caution to those who may want to join their ranks: Executive coaching, they say, is not the place for psychologists with no particular interest in business.

"You need to have some passion and respect and understanding for business and organizations," says Shullman. As an example, she says, the coach needs to understand the demands of the leadership roles from first-line supervision to middle management to the top executive.

Lloyd Brotman, Ph.D., who heads a Philadelphia consulting firm, adds that coaching requires solid grounding in the context of business, not just in terms of personal adjustment. And Bruce Peltier, Ph.D., author of *The Psychology of Executive Coaching,* stresses that a novice must come to understand not just business, but business people: "They move fast and they keep score—using money. It may not be everyone's cup of tea."

Meanwhile for those with the interest, there is no universally accepted certification for executive coaching. Nor are there standard definitions of coaching or regulations governing good practice. Anybody can claim to be a coach, and more people from many fields, particularly M.B.A.s, are becoming coaches, says psychologist Mary Kralj, Ph.D., who has coached for 12 years.

In fact, executive coaching is a "huge umbrella term," Tippins explains, so it's important for psychologists who coach to communicate with businesses on exactly what types of problems they are qualified to work on. A company may want a coach to counsel executives on their problems, to advise executives on organizational structure and design, or help executives motivate and manage problem employees—a wide range of issues that demand different skills, she says.

"Practice in the area in which you are trained," she stresses. Just as psychologists with industrial/organizational expertise may not be qualified to counsel executives on psychological problems, some practitioners may not be qualified to advise on designing a more efficient organization. "You have to say what you are capable of and what you are not, and not have the client figure it out," she adds.

WAYS TO SAMPLE THE FIELD

Getting started in coaching requires some additional learning for any psychologist, say coaching experts. "No one specialty in psychology may fully prepare someone to do executive coaching," explains Shullman. "If you're coming from a clinical background, there is a need to get experience with organizational behavior and issues as well as business context training, while those from the I/O end need an understanding of a range of clinical and developmental kinds of issues."

Psychologists who want to explore executive coaching can get a taste by attending the expanding number of continuing-education programs being offered on the topic. Kralj suggests getting involved with organizations that have a stake in coaching, such as APA's Divs. 13 (Society of Consulting Psychology) and 14 (Society for Industrial and Organizational Psychology). In addition, more extensive programs have been established. A number of psychologist-coaches got training at the Center for Creative Leadership, in Greensboro, N.C., for example. Brotman advises it helps to be acquainted with business professionals, just to understand the mindset. A number of psychologists suggest joining a Rotary or other business club both to learn and to make contacts.

"There really isn't one way to go about becoming an executive coach, but there are definitely requirements that every coach should have," says Shullman.

The most important one, according to Tippins, is hands-on experience that's supervised by a seasoned coach who can provide evaluation and feedback. Tippins got guidance by interning at a large corporation under several I/O psychologists. Kralj went to business school and became a manager herself before joining a consulting firm. To gain such practical experience, Shullman suggests practitioners contact consulting firms or psychologist-coaches who they might apprentice with.

Coaches also add that, as their careers progress, it's essential to keep up to date with the latest in both psychology and business.

Wasylyshyn has words of inspiration for psychologists who may want to explore the field: Coaching is more than just a business opportunity for psychologists, she says. It's an opportunity for psychology to help humanize the workplace at a time when it has become very Darwinian.

(reprinted with permission from Foxhall, 2002).

PSYCHOLOGISTS IN ACADEMIA

CHAPTER GUIDE

A CAREER AS A PROFESSOR

ACTIVITIES AND PROFESSIONAL
RESPONSIBILITIES

ADVANTAGES AND DISADVANTAGES
TO A CAREER AS A PROFESSOR

A CAREER IN RESEARCH

ACADEMIA

INDUSTRY

GOVERNMENT

SOCIAL SERVICE AGENCIES AND
NONPROFITS

**PREPARATION FOR A TEACHING
AND RESEARCH CAREER**

RECOMMENDED READINGS

WEB RESOURCES

**PROFILE 7.1: RICHARD M.
MCFALL, PH.D.**

**PROFILE 7.2: PETER J. SNYDER,
PH.D.**

Did you know that 40% of psychologists are found in academia (American Psychological Association, 1999)? Most students easily envision the academic settings in which psychologists work. Though you're familiar with the role of professor, do you really know all the things that professors do? In psychology, we talk a lot about research, but do you know what a career in research is like? This chapter will provide answers to these questions and help you to learn about academic careers as professors and researchers.

A CAREER AS A PROFESSOR

Though we're all familiar with professors, most of us underestimate the variety of activities in which professors engage. It's a life full of lazy afternoons peppered with occasional lectures to rapt students, right? Think again! Faculty positions are very competitive to secure and retain. While a master's degree will enable you to teach college courses, primarily as an adjunct (part-time professor) or at a community college, understand that most college teaching positions in psychology are held by doctoral degree holders. A doctoral degree affords the greatest opportunities for employment, mobility, and advancement as a faculty member at a college or university (Actkinson, 2000; Lloyd, 2000).

Activities and Professional Responsibilities

So what do professors do? Sure they spend time in class, lecturing, facilitating discussions, and helping students learn about their field, but a career as a professor entails more than classroom duty. There are three facets to a professor's work: teaching, research, and service (to both the campus and community). In addition, some professors also maintain an independant, clinical practice.

Day-to-day activities vary among individual professors as well as the types of colleges or universities where they are employed. There are several types of colleges and universities. Community colleges and liberal arts colleges tend to focus heavily on teaching such that faculty often teach between three and five courses per semester, as well as engage in service to the institution and community, leaving little time to conduct research or engage in scholarly writing. At the other extreme are research universities, large schools with prestigious graduate programs where faculty teach only one or two courses per semester. Instead, faculty focus heavily on research because they are judged on their reputations as scholars; teaching and service matter less to their professional advancement (but are expected) (Veslind, 2000). Many 4-year universities fall somewhere in between the two extremes and encourage faculty to actively engage in all three areas: research, teaching, and service. So, even within academia, there are several career tracks for psychologists.

Teach. A professor's work in teaching extends far from the classroom. Preparation requires a great deal of time and effort. Before each class professors usually read several chapters and journal articles in addition to what they've assigned students; they take notes, and prepare overheads, activities, and discussion questions. Preparation is always critical as the field is forever changing and remaining current is a challenge. Professors who teach three, four, or even five courses per semester may find that preparation takes most of their time, especially in the early years of a career (Roediger, 1997). Teaching isn't over when a professor leaves the classroom because he or she also grades papers, writes letters of recommendation for students, meets with students to answer questions and discuss course content and professional issues, and advises students on career choices.

Clinical and counseling psychology faculty, especially those who teach in a graduate program, may also engage in a unique teaching activity called clinical supervision. Clinical and counseling psychology students must learn the practice activities of psychologists: how to conduct psychological assessments, diagnose psychological disorders, design and implement interventions, and conduct therapy. Faculty must supervise clinical and counseling students' activities in applied settings to help them learn clinical skills and to protect clients by ensuring that students are skilled and act in the best interest of clients. Providing clinical supervision entails mentoring students as they cope with challenging tasks. As you might imagine, clinical supervision is a time-consuming responsibility, but also very rewarding .

Research. Professors often divide their time among multiple research tasks. For example, this week I've spent time writing this book, revising an article for submission to a journal, planning a research project that I will conduct with one of my students, and conducting statistical analyses for a presentation that I will make in a couple of weeks. Other research tasks in which professors engage include writing grant proposals, searching the literature, reading research articles, meeting with student research assistants, advising students on their research, serving as peer reviewers for articles submitted to psychology journals and research proposals submitted to funding agencies, and preparing or giving talks at professional meetings. As a student of psychology, you've learned that a research study often leads to more questions than it answers, so research projects can quickly snowball into multifaceted careers.

Service. Faculty engage in service to their departments, the institution, and the community. In other words, they help the department, campus, and surrounding community through advising, sitting on the many committees that run the university, and engaging in administrative work. For example, professors sit on committees to hire new professors and administrators, to evaluate student applicants, and to help determine the institution's budget. Psychology professors often participate on boards and advise social service agencies in the community. Some faculty develop programs in the school systems or devote time to giving presentations to students, parents, teachers, and community leaders.

Clinical Practice. Most university faculty are evaluated on the "big three" —research, teaching, and service; however, clinical and counseling psychology faculty often engage in clinical practice in university and off-campus settings (Bootzin, 2004). Some faculty develop small independent practices as a way of maintaining their clinical skills. Others develop clinics to serve as training clinics for students. Many departments encourage clinical and counseling psychology faculty to remain active in their field and engage in practice activities in order to enrich their teaching with applied examples.

Advantages and Disadvantages to a Career as a Professor

A career as a professor offers a variety of advantages and challenges. Perhaps the greatest advantages are academic freedom, and the autonomy and flexibility of academic life. Academic freedom means that professors they may conduct whatever research interests them and may "teach the truth as they see it" (Vesilind, 2000, p. 10). In other words, professors choose how to teach their course content. They choose texts, reading assignments, grading, and evaluation procedures, based on their beliefs about how to best teach their field. Aside from class time, professors' schedules tend to be flexible. Most develop work habits that fit their lives, allowing time to pick up children from school, spend time with their families, and complete preparation and writing in the late evenings or early mornings.

Tenure is another advantage to a career as a professor. Tenure is intended to provide complete academic freedom because it prevents professors from being fired for airing unpopular views or pursuing controversial research. Professors with documented teaching histories, excellent student evaluations, publications, campus committee work, and outreach to the community earn tenure and the associated job security. There are also many intangible benefits to a career as a professor, such as the excitement of discovery and innovation, as well as the rewards of imparting knowledge and introducing students to a life of the mind (Roediger, 1997; Vesilind, 2000). Personally, I've found that working closely with students offers tremendous rewards: talking with them, discussing difficult concepts, conducting research with them, and watching them graduate and move on to their own careers. As a professor, you touch others' lives— and make a difference.

In addition to many advantages, professorial careers also entail challenges. Research and professorial careers in academia entail long hours, especially in research-oriented institutions in which one must "publish or perish." Publish or perish is a dramatic way of explaining that some university settings require faculty to publish many quality articles in prestigious journals in order to earn tenure. In recent years, publishing has become more important at all types of institutions, even at teaching-oriented institutions (Salzinger, 1995). Professors, therefore, spend many evenings in the lab or at the computer completing research or writing articles based on their research. The tremendous amounts of time invested in conducting and publishing research can strain other areas of a professor's life. Finding time for everything, and balancing work and play, is stressful. Though conducting and writing for publication entail long hours and "brain drain," it's rewarding to contribute to the field and generate new knowledge. The wonderment of discovery makes the personal and professional strain worthwhile.

An important disadvantage to choosing a career as a professor is that academic positions are scarce. The job market is very competitive; there aren't a lot of academic positions available. Some applicants spend several years searching for a job, working as postdoctoral researchers, in one-year instructor appointments, or adjunct faculty positions. Serious applicants don't limit themselves to searching for positions in particular geographic locations, but are prepared to move wherever the job takes them. Finally, as shown by the salaries in Table 7.1, a career as a professor will not make you rich.

| TABLE 7.1 | MEAN SALARIES FOR PROFESSORS |

(Adapted from Chronicle of Higher Education, 2003)

Institution and Position	Average Annual Salary ($)
Doctoral institutions	
Professor	97,910
Associate professor	67,043
Assistant professor	57,131
Comprehensive institutions (Master's level)	
Professor	75,334
Associate professor	59,326
Assistant professor	48,965
Baccalaureate institutions	
Professor	69,598
Associate professor	53,575
Assistant professor	44,700

A CAREER IN RESEARCH

Some clinical and counseling psychologists seek careers in academia at universities, government, private organizations, and in industry. Each of these settings is different in terms of the emphases of the research, the autonomy afforded researchers, and salaries (as seen in Table 7.2).

TABLE 7.2   MEDIAN SALARIES FOR DOCTORAL-LEVEL CAREERS IN RESEARCH WITH 2–4 YEARS OF EXPERIENCE

(Adapted from Singleton, Tate, & Randall, 2003; Williams, Wicherski, & Kohout, 2000)

	Median Annual Salary ($)
University research center	45,000
Private research organization	57,000
Government research organization	57,000
Nonprofit organization	55,000
Industry	74,000

Academia

Many clinical and counseling psychologists work in university settings as research scientists. Clinical and counseling psychologists conduct research on a wide range of topics, such as factors that contribute to the development of eating disorders, personality development, influences on help-seeking behaviors, career development, causes, diagnosis, and treatment of pathology, influences on psychological health, and more.

A research career in academia offers a flexible schedule and is prestigious. Research scientists gain independence and autonomy as they progress in their careers. By writing and winning research grants, researchers are able to fund and study problems of their choosing. With advancement, research scientists take on supervisory roles, run their own labs, and train graduate students and postdoctoral students. There are also opportunities for travel and contact with the public through speaking at conferences, consulting, and writing for the popular press (Bartholomew, 2001a). A disadvantage of a research career in academia is the competition. Generally, academic positions that don't require teaching can be difficult to obtain. Applicants may need to be able to relocate for available positions. Also, most research scientists at least partially support their salaries by applying for and obtaining funding via grants. Grant writing is challenging, and it is stressful to be responsible for ensuring that the research lab secures enough funds to keep your job. If you seek a research career, be prepared to put in many long hours.

Industry

Some clinical and counseling psychologists conduct research in business and industry—conducting surveys of consumer opinion, for example. Others who work for pharmaceutical companies might test the effectiveness of drugs for treating psychological disorders or work as statisticians, analyzing the data from a variety of research projects. In industry, the goal of research is to promote the success of the company, to benefit the company, employees, and shareholders (Bartholomew, 2001b).

In industry, research is fast paced because information must be gathered quickly to help create and sell products. Teams conduct the research, enabling greater productivity. In addition, psychologists in business and industry settings tend to have access to more funding than do those in academia, meaning that they tend to work with newer and more sophisticated equipment. The primary drawback of conducting research in business and industry is that your research questions are assigned based on the needs of the company, not necessarily on your interests. An important benefit of working in industry is the contact with people of diverse fields and educational backgrounds. Other benefits are the high salaries and regular work schedule; in business and industry, your weekends generally are your own.

Government

Although research psychologists engage in similar activities regardless of work setting—whether universities, industry, or government—the three settings differ in terms of the autonomy afforded researchers. Similar to scientists in industry, those employed by the government and military usually examine research questions not conceived by them (Herrman, 1997). Instead, they examine questions that are created by politicians and policy makers, designed to promote the security and well being of the nation's people. Because policy decisions hold long-term implications for people, research questions tend to be complex, sensitive, and require extensive coordination with multiple federal agencies (Copper, 1997).

An advantage of a research career in government is that you'll be exposed to many different projects. Unlike academia, where researchers spend a career focused on a particular research problem or area, research psychologists in government work on a diverse range of projects and become generalists. Most research projects initiated by the government are short in duration (about 1 year to complete) because the research is intended to help resolve practical problems. Also, shifts in public opinion and interest lead political leaders to eliminate some projects and initiate new ones; whether this is an advantage or disadvantage perhaps depends on your interest in the project.

If you're interested in a research career in government, be prepared to engage in lots of supervisory work because contractors conduct much of the hands-on work under supervision by government researchers. This enables government researchers to work on multiple projects at once and not become overly involved in any one project. Like industry, government research involves working on a team because the research topics that the government is interested in are applied; requiring creativity and planning by an interdisciplinary team of researchers consisting of psychologists, sociologists, statisticians, computer scientists, economists, and more.

Social Service Agencies and Nonprofits

Clinical and counseling psychologists employed at social service or nonprofit agencies conduct research to assess and improve the agency's programs and often write grants to help fund the agency. Social service and nonprofit agencies often are contracted by the government to conduct policy analyses, literature reviews, and research to improve decision making by political leaders and consumers. A psychologist at such an agency might examine the effectiveness of new drug control interventions like mandatory minimum sanctions, residential and group home treatments for youthful offenders identified as drug users, and school-based prevention programs.

The primary benefit of working in a nonprofit or social service agency is that your time is focused on research that may lead to social change. Such agencies tend to conduct interdisciplinary research, enabling research psychologists to work with a diverse range of specialists of other fields. Though the salaries at nonprofit and social service agencies tend to be lower than in other research settings, the research often directly benefits consumers and families.

Preparation for a Teaching and Research Career

If you're interested in a career in academia or other research settings, understand that the doctoral degree offers the most flexibility, opportunities for advancement, and opportunities to serve as the primary investigator of federal grants (Lloyd, 2000). Chapter 7 discusses graduate study in clinical and counseling psychology. Research psychologists in academia often complete 2 to 3 years of postdoctoral training after obtaining the doctoral degree. To be competitive for research positions within academic and nonacademic settings, hone your skills in research methods and statistics while in graduate school, seek additional research experience, and try to publish your first article as a graduate student (Copper, 1997).

For a career as a professor, also seek teaching experience (but not at the exclusion of research experience—try to gain competence in both, a daunting task indeed). Seek a graduate program that helps to prepare students for the teaching aspects of the professorate. Training in pedagogy is essential (Kuther, 2002). Successful professors master the techniques of their trade and learn how to compose lectures, lead discussions, create syllabi, enhance student learning through effective use of the blackboard, overheads, or PowerPoint presentations, and model best practices for interacting with students and handling disagreements. Many graduate programs have seminars and courses in how to teach. Preparing Future Faculty, a program designed to prepare aspiring academics for the variety of teaching, research, and service roles entailed in the professorate, has also created a wealth of resources and a website available at http://www.preparing-faculty.org/ (American Psychological Association, 2001; Preparing Future Faculty, n.d.). Seek practical experience as a teaching assistant or adjunct professor at your university or a nearby college. You can also volunteer to teach a class or two for your primary instructors or for instructors teaching courses in your area of interest. Most importantly, find a mentor in graduate school who can help you with these essential aspects of training.

RECOMMENDED READINGS

Balster, R. L. (1995). An interesting career in psychology: A research psychologist in a medical school. *Psychological Science Agenda.* Retrieved on February 1, 2002, at http://www.apa.org/science/ic-balster.html

Cohen, L., Morgan, R., DeLillo, D., & Flores, L. Y. (2003). Why was my major professor so busy? Establishing an academic career while pursuing applied work. *Professional Psychology: Research and Practice, 34,* 88–94.

Keller, P. A. (1994). *Academic paths: Career decisions and experiences of psychologists.* Mahwah, NJ: Erlbaum.

Rheingold, H. L. (1994). *The psychologist's guide to an academic career.* Washington, DC: American Psychological Association.

Sternberg, R. J. (1997). *Career paths in psychology: Where your degree can take you.* Washington, DC: American Psychological Association.

Vesilind, P. A. (2000). *So you want to be a professor? A handbook for graduate students.* Thousand Oaks, CA: Sage.

WEB RESOURCES

Career Development Center for Postdocs and Junior Faculty
http://nextwave.sciencemag.org/feature/careercenter.shtml

Getting Beyond the Academic Gatekeepers: The Tenure Process
  http://www.apa.org/apags/profdev/abttenure.html

Office of Teaching Resources in Psychology
  http://www.lemoyne.edu/OTRP/index.html

Preparing Future Faculty
  http://www.preparing-faculty.org/

Society for the Teaching of Psychology
  http://teachpsych.lemoyne.edu/

PROFILE 7.1: RICHARD M. MCFALL, PH.D.

Dr. McFall is a Professor of Psychology at Indiana University. He is an expert in the area of interpersonal competence, and his widely cited research has appeared in numerous journals and books read by clinical psychologists. In addition to his research pursuits, Dr. McFall has taught and trained many clinical psychologists through his roles as faculty member and Director of Clinical Training. Finally, Dr. McFall is recognized as influential in establishing the clinical science model of training. He served as the president of the Academy of Psychological Clinical Science from 1995 to 1998. Dr. McFall was kind enough to respond to the following questions we posed.

What originally got you interested in the field of clinical psychology?

As an undergraduate at DePauw University, I was an art major until my junior year, when it occurred to me to ask my professor what I might be able to do with a degree in art. Among other things, he suggested that I might become an account executive in advertising. He suggested that I take a psychology course to learn what motivated people to buy things. So, I went over to the psychology department. Of course, I had to take prerequisites (introductory, statistics, experimental, and so on) before I could take the "good stuff," and before I knew it, I was a psychology major. At the start of my senior year, still intending to go into advertising, I took a clinical psychology course taught by John Exner (the world-famous Rorschach expert) devoted primarily to projective tests. Exner encouraged me to apply to graduate school in clinical psychology, and gave me a list of the prospective graduate programs, all psychodynamically oriented. As I began filling out applications, my roommate's father, who happened to be a psychologist, visited campus. He suggested that I apply to Ohio State University (where he got his degree). I did, more or less as a "backup." OSU admitted me and offered a generous assistantship—more than any other program. Being financially independent and in debt, I accepted OSU's offer. As it turned out, the OSU clinical program was one of the best in the country at the time. It had a very strong scientific emphasis. I quickly learned that I had entered graduate school for illusory reasons; however, the research orientation of OSU's program was compelling, and I soon developed an interest in clinical psychology as a science.

Describe what activities you are involved in as a clinical psychologist.

First and foremost I am a teacher. For most of my career, I have taught Introduction to Clinical Psychology to advanced undergraduates and Clinical Psychology to first-year graduate students. My goal in both classes is to teach the students to think skeptically and critically about the problems that are the primary focus in clinical psychology. I also teach a clinical practicum for advanced doctoral students in which we review the empirical research evidence on the effectiveness of different methods of treating persons with obsessive-compulsive disorders (OCD), apply the best of the available methods to OCD clients in our own clinic, and evaluate the results of our interventions.

I am also an active researcher. The common theme of my research is interpersonal competence—how to define and measure it, how to predict and promote it, and the factors that lead to incompetence. Competence and psychopathology can be seen as opposite sides of the same coin. Psychopathology can be viewed as a lack of competence in one or more critical areas of functioning. To understand the etiology of psychopathology, then, clinical psychologists might want to understand the nature and origins of competence. My research draws heavily on the knowledge and methods of psychology as a whole, especially cognitive science and neuroscience. This means that I must be an active student of the discipline.

Another facet of my professional life is my involvement in administrative and service roles. I have been director of the clinical training program at Indiana University; have been on the board of directors of the local community mental health center; have served on editorial boards of journals; and have been active in professional organizations at the national level. Virtually all of my professional efforts, in one way or another, are devoted to differentiating science from pseudoscience within clinical psychology, and to promoting clinical psychology as a science.

What are your particular areas of expertise or interest?

I've already described my content focus in research: interpersonal competence. In pursuing this interest, I have studied a variety of specific clinical problems and populations—including shy college men and women; nonassertive individuals; persons suffering from schizophrenia, depression, OCD, eating disorders, and addiction to tobacco; adolescent boys and girls identified as juvenile delinquents; and men who are sexually coercive toward women. My research across these problem areas has been characterized by an emphasis on conceptual and measurement issues. Recent work, in particular, has explored the use of concepts and methods adapted from cognitive science and neuroscience. My goal is to build better theoretical and quantitative models of clinically relevant phenomena.

What are the future trends you see for clinical psychology?

Clinical training programs that continue to have a strong "practice" focus (whether they identify themselves as Psy.D. programs or scientist-practitioner Ph.D. programs) are ignoring the dramatic changes currently taking place within the mental health field (increasingly called the behavioral health field). As health care in the United States shifts from the traditional fee-for-service model to the managed care model, clinical psychologists are losing their role as primary care providers. The reasons are obvious. Two to three social workers can be hired for the price of one psychologist. If the research evidence shows no difference in treatment outcome between doctoral-level clinical psychologists and master's-level social workers, then the cost-conscious managed care systems will hire social workers, rather than psychologists, to provide most mental health services. One feature distinguishes some doctoral-level clinical psychologists from most other mental health specialists, however; this is the psychologist's research training, or special preparation for the role of research scientist. Only those clinical training programs that have maintained and strengthened the Ph.D.'s traditional focus on scientific research training are preparing their students for a viable future in the changing mental health care field.

(Reprinted with permission from Trull & Phares, 2001.)

PROFILE 7.2: PETER J. SNYDER, PH.D.

As a young child I decided that, if I was unable to pursue a career as a helicopter-jumping wilderness firefighter, then I would I model after my father and obtain a Ph.D. in psychology and neuroscience. Over time I decided against a career as a firefighter, and I have pursued one in psychology. In my junior year at the University of Michigan, while completing an honors thesis on a topic in behavioral neuroendocrinology, I took an "Introduction to Human Neuropsychology" course offered by the professor who had supervised my father's Ph.D. dissertation about 20 years beforehand, Dr. Charles Butters. Charlie's course convinced me that it was possible to conduct elegant and innovative human cognitive neuroscience research, and so I set my sights on the field of human neuropsychology. For the next 3 years, I spent almost all academic holidays and summer vacation time in Connecticut as a student under the supervision of Dr. Robert A. Novelly (Comprehensive Epilepsy Center at Yale and the West Haven VAMC). I remember the day that I first watched Bob conduct an intracarotid sodium amobarbital test ("Wada Test") on a patient being considered for surgical resection of a focal epileptogenic lesion—it was at that moment that I knew I had to become both a clinical neuropsychologist and a researcher.

I completed my Ph.D. at Michigan State University under the primary supervision of Professor Lauren Julius Harris. Lauren taught me how to be careful and conscientious as a scientist, how to teach others, and how to write with some skill. He was a wonderful mentor, to whom I thank for ensuring that I remained fully committed to the "Boulder Model". I received my Ph.D. in 1992, after completing the Clinical Neuropsychology Internship at the Long Island Jewish Medical Center (Albert Einstein College of Medicine), and I remained there, as a postdoctoral fellow, to pursue studies of speech and language disorders in epilepsy using quantitative MRI morphometric techniques.

In 1994 I moved to the Department of Neurology at MCP Hahnemann School of Medicine (Pittsburgh campus), to become the principal neuropsychologist for the Comprehensive Epilepsy Center at Allegheny General Hospital in Pittsburgh, PA. I was appointed the Director of the Division of Behavioral Neurology, and in 1998 I became Associate Professor of Neurology. I had the unique experience of being the only Ph.D. in my department at a large university medical center, as well as being the only clinical Ph.D. in a private practice group with five neurologists. This was a fantastic arrangement, and I enjoyed great opportunities for professional growth and development as a professor and researcher, as a clinician with a strong background in neurology, and as a manager.

My career took an abrupt turn when, a little more than four years ago, my fiancée was placed in an OB-gyn residency program in Connecticut. Within six months of receiving a long-dreamt-of academic promotion, I moved to Connecticut to accept a clinical research position at the largest R&D campus for the pharmaceutical company Pfizer, Inc. To the best of my knowledge, I am the sole neuropsychologist employed within Pfizer's R&D division, on any of its research campuses. My principal roles at Pfizer are: (1) to evaluate and/or discover new brain imaging and non-imaging neurophysiologic methods for detecting and tracking early CNS disease progression; and (2) to serve as an internal consultant on the appropriate, ethical, and rational use of neuropsychological instrumentation. I am also an Adjunct Professor of Psychology at the University of Connecticut (Storrs, CT), where I supervise doctoral students and teach the graduate core course in cognitive neuroscience.

The transition from clinical practice and an academic medical research career to a career in the pharmaceutical industry was challenging. There are aspects of clinical practice that I miss, but the opportunities at Pfizer for innovative research are enormous. I am fortunate to work in a setting that allows substantial creative freedom and the ability to expand my own research group using a largely academic model. A company like Pfizer possesses the resources that are required to tackle the complex problem of developing novel (sensitive and specific) biomarkers of CNS disease progression and/or treatment response. Most of my research, in some way, contributes to the short- or medium-range goals for the company to develop effective and safe pharmacologic treatments for a variety of neurologic illnesses. At Pfizer, I am privileged to work closely with extremely bright and talented individuals who span numerous scientific and medical disciplines. Just as important, my students are benefiting tremendously from access to the vast array of research and educational opportunities at Pfizer. I suspect that all pharmaceutical companies support their scientists' efforts to remain as active contributors to their respective fields. I am encouraged to continue my pre-existing collaborative research relationships, to build new ones, and to maintain an active role in my own field. Not long ago it was assumed that leaving academia for industry was akin to committing "professional suicide." In my experience, this old view is entirely inaccurate. It is possible to enjoy an exciting research career in a pharmaceutical R&D setting, and to mix quality research with business opportunities that may greatly enhance management and leadership skills. Since joining a pharmaceutical company I have had more opportunities to continue to teach, to supervise graduate students and postdoctoral fellows, and to edit, write and publish than I can possibly keep up with. I have stopped trying to accurately predict what twists and turns my career path will take. I tell my students that if they enjoy their work and strive for excellence, then unexpected opportunities will emerge that may radically alter the career trajectory they had anticipated.

(Reprinted with permission from the Winter 2002 issue of Psychological Science Agenda.)

Is a Career in Clinical or Counseling Psychology for You?

Chapter Guide

Master's Degrees in Clinical and Counseling Psychology

What Can You Do with a Master's Degree?

What Does a Master's Degree Entail?

Doctoral Degrees

Training Models

Ph.D. vs Psy.D.

What Does a Doctoral Degree Entail?

Postdoctoral Specialization

Licensure

Advancing Your Career: What You Can Do Now

Become Known by Your Professors

Obtain Research Experience

Obtain Applied Experience

Begin Preparing for Graduate Study

Recommended Readings

Web Resources

Throughout this book we've discussed some of the many career paths that clinical and counseling psychologists travel. All of the careers described in this book require a graduate degree. In this chapter, we take a closer look at graduate training in clinical and counseling psychology. What graduate training options exist? What are the steps entailed in becoming a psychologist? What can you do now, as a student, to prepare for a career in clinical or counseling psychology?

MASTER'S DEGREES IN CLINICAL AND COUNSELING PSYCHOLOGY

Much confusion exists regarding the master's degree in psychology (Actkinson, 2000). Students and their advisors often lack information about this degree and the career preparation it offers. Regardless, the master's degree in psychology is popular, with about 13,000 conferred each year.

What Can You Do with a Master's Degree?

Why get a master's degree in clinical or counseling psychology? What can you do with it? Entry-level positions in each of the careers described in this book are possible with a master's degree. For example, a master's degree qualifies one to teach in higher education settings; however, recognize that competition for positions as faculty at colleges and universities is fierce. Although you may be hired as an adjunct with a master's degree, full-time positions are often held by doctoral-level psychologists.

A master's degree in clinical or counseling psychology will enable you to practice psychology in a variety of settings. Because studies have been inconclusive regarding therapeutic outcomes and level of training of the practitioner (e.g., Christensen & Jacobson, 1994; Seligman, 1995; Stein & Lambert, 1995), some psychologists argue that a form of licensure should be extended to master's-level psychologists (Hays-Thomas, 2000). Currently, however, a doctoral degree is required for licensure. In many states, a master's-level psychologist can be certified as a psychological assistant and conduct all of the direct service activities discussed in this book. The caveat is that master's-level psychologists and psychological assistants must be supervised by doctoral-level psychologists. Some clinical and counseling master's programs meet the requirements to seek licensure as counselors or marriage and family therapists, enabling independent practice (Levant, Moldawsky, & Stigall, 2000). If your goal is to set up an independent or private practice, carefully research your options beforehand so that you're not disappointed later.

Many individuals with master's degrees have rewarding careers in research in academic, public health, and social policy settings. Like the other careers we've discussed, the doctoral degree will provide you with a greater variety of career opportunities. Particularly in academic settings, the doctoral degree offers more flexibility, opportunities for advancement, and opportunities to serve as the primary investigator of federal grants (Lloyd, 2000).

Unlike the other career options we've discussed, a master's degree can provide excellent preparation for a career as an executive coach, if one obtains the necessary experience in business. If you have interests and experience in business, a master's degree in clinical or counseling psychology will provide the applied skills to become a coach. However, successful coaches have extensive training and experience with organizations. Frequently executive coaches obtain master's degrees in industrial or organizational psychology or become coaches after developing successful careers in business settings.

What Does a Master's Degree Entail?

A master's degree typically requires two years of full-time study to complete. At first, you'll enroll in classes, much like your undergraduate courses. Some of the courses will be very applied. For example, courses in assessment will require a great deal of hands-on activity. You'll also complete a specified number of supervised practice hours as part of your degree. You may also complete a master's thesis, or an extended research paper. In your master's thesis, you will pose a research question, review the relevant literature, and design and carry out a research study to address your question. Some master's programs offer alternatives to the master's thesis, such as qualifying examinations or other written projects that are less rigorous than theses.

DOCTORAL DEGREES

Training Models

There are three basic models of doctoral training: clinician-scientist, scientist-practitioner, and professional psychologist-practitioner. Choose a training model that fits your interests—and then choose programs that emulate your chosen model. Most psychologists engage in the same type of activities that they experienced in their graduate program of study, so pick a training model that will prepare you for the career you desire.

The clinician-scientist model is designed to create scientists who will make new discoveries and advance psychological knowledge. The clnician-scientist model is the oldest training model and it characterizes most programs in the core academic areas of psychology such as experimental, social/personality, quantitative, physiological, and developmental psychology. Graduates trained as clinical scientists conduct original research, teach, and write about their research findings. The emphases of training include experimental methods, methodological skills, and content knowledge. Graduates trained as clinician scientists tend to be employed as college and university professors, and researchers in universities, government, and industry settings. Given the applied emphasis of clinical and counseling psychology, the majority of graduate programs do not adopt the clnician-scientist model of training.

Instead, graduate programs in clinical and counseling psychology, specifically Ph.D. programs in clinical and counseling psychology, tend to adopt the scientist-practitioner model of graduate training, which seeks to mold students into scholars who integrate their research training with applied work. The scientist-practitioner model of training is often referred to as the Boulder Model, after the city in which the first national training conference on clinical psychology was held (Boulder, Colorado). At this conference, it was decided that clinical psychologists should receive dual emphasis in training to develop both research and clinical competencies. Therefore, scientist-practitioners are trained in research and methodology, like research scientists, but also receive training in application, combined with applied experiences through internships and practica. Graduates trained in the scientist-practitioner model are employed by hospitals and clinical practices, teach in colleges and universities, and own private practices. The extent to which a particular psychologist engages in both research and practice depends on his or her job setting and commitment to research; many practicing clinicians do little to no research.

Graduate programs oriented toward the professional psychologist/practitioner model, specifically Psy.D. programs, train students to provide psychological services. This model is sometimes referred to as the scholar-practitioner model, or more commonly, the Vail model, after the conference in Vail, Colorado. At this meeting it was decided that psychology had matured enough to warrant the creation of degrees that are explicitly professional in nature, similar to professional programs in law, medicine, and dentistry (Norcross & Castle, 2002). Therefore, professional psychologist/practitioner training emphasizes clinical practice over research. Graduates are trained to be consumers of research rather than producers of it—and tend to be employed in practice settings such as hospitals, clinics, and private practice.

Ph.D. vs Psy.D.

After examining the training models in psychology, the differences between the Ph.D. and Psy.D. should be more clear. Both degrees will enable you to practice psychology as a licensed psychologist. As we've discussed, Ph.D. programs provide a greater focus on research skills than do Psy.D. programs. Students earning a Ph.D. complete a doctoral dissertation based in empirical research whereas oftentimes only a written project is necessary to complete requirements for the Psy.D. However, students in Psy.D. programs often have many more hours of clinical experience than do students in Ph.D. programs. So how do you know which degree is for you?

What do you hope to be doing in 10 years? Although programs offering both the Ph.D. and Psy.D. train students to be clinicians, only Ph.D. programs train students to be scientists. So, if you're interested in becoming a practitioner and seek a program that emphasizes practice, the Psy.D. may fit your needs. However, if you're interested in developing your skills as a scientific researcher as well as your clinical skills, then the Ph.D. is in order. Which degree you choose is your decision, but recognize that there are no differences in applicant quality between students in Psy.D. versus Ph.D. programs though Psy.D. prgrams have higher acceptance rates(see Norcross et al., 1998). In other words, both options are highly competitive.

What Does a Doctoral Degree Entail?

A doctoral degree in psychology usually entails 5 to 7 years of graduate study, including research experience and supervised applied experience. During the first few years of graduate school, you'll take classes. If you're in a Ph.D. program, you'll probably work with a faculty member on his or her research and may even work as a teaching assistant. Your job during graduate school is to learn how to be a professional and create your own program of research. You'll read outside of class, consider research questions, and begin your own research program under your mentor's supervision. If you're in a Psy.D. program, you will find that they will spend time outside of class in several semester or year long practica—where you will get supervised experience in therapy.

Programs vary, but most students are required to complete comprehensive examinations before they can begin working on their doctoral dissertations or doctoral projects. Comprehensive exams are just that—written and sometimes oral examinations that require that you become well read and up-to-date with the latest research and theories in your field.

The biggest hurdle for most graduate students in the dissertation. The dissertation is an in-depth research study that addresses a question pertinent to your research program and demonstrates your ability to undertake scholarship in your field. The Ph.D. dissertation requires that students complete an independent empirical research project that reflects a substantial contribution to the field and demonstrates the ability to build theory, test ideas, and/or discover new knowledge. Most students take at least 2 years to complete their dissertations. The Psy.D. prepares graduates to be consumers of research, or to understand and apply research rather than generate it. Because of the applied and professional orientation of Psy.D. programs, dissertations typically do not entail empirical research. Instead, the Psy.D. dissertation demonstrates the student's ability to read and interpret a body of research literature and apply it in practical situations. For example, the dissertation may be a critique of the research literature in a specific area of psychology, a thorough analysis of a case using the psychological literature as a theoretical and empirical framework, or planning and evaluating a prevention or intervention program.

Post-Doctoral Specialization

After earning their doctorates, many psychologists enter post-doctoral training and internship programs that permit them to gain knowledge and experience in specialty areas of psychology, like forensic, police, and health psychology. Training in clinical and counseling psychology provides a base set of practitioner tools; however, many psychologists are interested in applying psychology to particular types of problems, clients, and settings. Some psychologists specialize in correctional psychology by completing internships within correctional settings. Others enroll in formal programs that permit them to learn setting-specific skills. For example, psychologists with forensic psychology interests might enter postdoctoral training programs affiliated with law schools, permitting them to obtain training in the relevant aspects of law. Look back through the career profiles presented in this book and you'll notice that many of the psychologists profiled have completed postdoctoral study in order to enhance their skills as psychologists and specialize in particular areas of interest.

LICENSURE

In order to practice psychology and to use the title "psychologist," you must obtain a license. Licensure is designed to protect the public by determining that only those with the proper credentials and experience practice psychology. In that vein, only licensed psychologists are eligible for third-party reimbursement (i.e., payment by insurance companies). Though all states have licensure requirements, there is a great deal of variability in eligibility criteria for licensure (Habben, 2003). Because licensure for each state applies only to that state (e.g., a New York license enables you to practice only in New York; if you move your practice to New Jersey, you must obtain a license to practice in New Jersey), learn about the licensure requirements for any and all of the states in which you may reside.

Despite variability, there are some similarities in licensure requirements across states. For example, all states require completion of a doctoral degree. Most states require that the doctoral degree is obtained in a program accredited by the American Psychological Association (APA), thereby certifying its rigor and training emphases, but it is possible in some states to seek licensure with a degree from a program that is not APA accredited as long as the specific educational criteria for licensure are met (review the required courses in your state). In addition to a doctoral degree, at least 2 years of supervised practice are required. Most students complete the first year as part of their degree requirements, the 1-year full-time internship (or a 2-year part-time internship) in which they receive supervision for providing psychological services (e.g., therapy, assessment, crisis intervention). After completion of the doctoral degree (including completion of the internship) the licensee must acquire an additional year of supervised experience. This experience can be in the form of a formalized postdoctoral program, but it can also be less structured (e.g., in a private practice setting) as long as it includes providing psychological services under the supervision of a doctoral-level licensed psychologist. Again, states vary in terms of the total number of supervised hours required; most range from 1,500 to 2,000 (Habben, 2003).

All states require a passing score on the Examination for Professional Practice in Psychology (EPPP), though the definition of "passing" varies by state. The EPPP is a standardized exam that assesses a variety of content areas pertinent to professional psychology: treatment/intervention, ethical/legal/professional issues, assessment and diagnosis, cognitive-affective bases of behavior, growth and lifespan development, social and multicultural bases of behavior, biological bases of behavior, and research methods. Some states also require a jurisprudence examination, which is a written test specific to the ethical code and licensure laws of each state. Thus, if you're applying for licensure in California, you will be asked questions regarding California law and ethical code, but if you're applying for licensure in New York, you'll answer questions about New York statutes and ethics code (Kuther & Morgan, 2004). Some states also require an additional oral examination in which licensees are presented with a case vignette and asked questions regarding diagnosis, treatment planning, and ethical concerns, as well as what multicultural issues might impact the case. Though it's a lengthy and challenging process, licensure has rewards: the ability to use the title of "psychologist" and practice indepedently, without supervision.

ADVANCING YOUR CAREER: WHAT YOU CAN DO NOW

So you'd like to enter the field of clinical or counseling psychology. Now what? What can you do now, as a student, to prepare yourself for a career in clinical or counseling psychology?

Become Known by Your Professors

Professors have much to offer you, but most students see their professors only in the classroom. Take the time to get to know your professors and you'll discover a host of professional development opportunities, such as those to get involved in research, learn about internships and practica, and get career advice and tips. How do you get to know professors? Talk to them after class. Stop by during office hours. Ask content-related questions and demonstrate your interest in their specialty.

Obtain Research Experience

Many practice-oriented students shy away from research. Don't! Research experience is critical to your applied career in psychology in at least two ways. First, research experience will help you gain entry to competitive graduate programs in clinical and counseling psychology. Second, engaging in research helps you to develop your scientific reasoning and critical thinking abilities—skills that are the mark of competent psychologists. Psychological practice requires research skills because when you work with a client, you tests hypotheses regarding the client's needs, and you systematically test hypotheses to determine the appropriate treatment. Also, practicing psychologists must remain current with the literature—and research skills make it easier to review and comprehend complicated journal articles.

Obtain research experience by assisting professors with their research or by developing an independent research project. Perform well in class and demonstrate motivation by making contact with your professors and being an active participant in the department. Approach faculty during their office hours and ask for information on who might be looking for research assistants. If you're interested in a particular faculty member's work, approach him or her and ask if you can help.

Obtain Applied Experience

Secure an internship or practicum for hands-on experience. Internships provide wonderful opportunities to apply what you've learned in the classroom to the real world, have learning experiences that you'd never obtain in a classroom setting, and explore potential careers. For example, do you really want to work with people? Your internship experiences may surprise you. This is critical especially if you're considering becoming a practicing clinical or counseling psychologist because such careers entail many interpersonal challenges. Psychological practice is not for everyone. In addition, applied experiences can help you to make contacts and your supervisor can provide a reference or recommendation for graduate study based on your performance. Learn about internship opportunities by asking faculty in your department. Also visit the career development center at your college and to learn about opportunities to gain hands-on experience.

Begin Preparing for Graduate Study

Graduate programs in clinical and counseling psychology are very competitive for admission. If you think that you'd like to become a clinical or counseling psychologist, don't delay in learning about the admissions process because successful applicants are those who begin considering their graduate school options and preparing early. For more information about graduate study in clinical and counseling psychology, and how to prepare, review the recommended readings and resources at the end of this chapter.

RECOMMENDED READINGS

American Psychological Association. (1994). *Getting in: A step-by-step plan for gaining admission to graduate school in psychology.* Washington, DC: Author.

American Psychological Association. (2001). *Graduate study in psychology: 2000 edition with 2001 addendum.* Washington, DC: Author.

Keith-Spiegel, P. & Wiederman, M. W. (2000). *Complete guide to graduate school admissions: Psychology, counseling, and related professions.* Mahwah, NJ: Erlbaum.

Kuther, T. L. (2003). *The psychology major's handbook.* Belmont, CA: Wadsworth.

Mayne, T. J., Norcross, J. G., & Sayette, M. A. (2000). *Insider's guide to graduate programs in clinical and counseling psychology.* New York: Guilford.

Palmer, C. A., & Baucom, D. H. (1999). Making the most of your clinical Ph.D.: Preparing for a successful career in an evolving and diversified profession. *The Clinical Psychologist, 52*(2), 7–17.

Prinstein, M. J., & Patterson, M. D. (2003). *The portable mentor: Expert guide to a successful career in psychology.* New York: Kluwer.

WEB RESOURCES

About Graduate School
    http://gradschool.about.co

Applying to Graduate School
    http://www.psichi.org/pubs/search.asp?category1=7

Early Career Psychologists
    http://www.apa.org/earlycareer/

Finding Opportunities to Get Involved in Research: Some Advice From the Students' Perspective
    http://psichi.org/pubs/articles/article_45.asp

Maximizing Undergraduate Opportunities: The Value of Research and Other Experiences
    http://psichi.org/pubs/articles/article_39.asp

What Does Your Transcript Say About You, and What Can You Do If It Says Things You Don't Like?
    http://psichi.org/pubs/articles/article_341.asp

References

Actkinson, T. R. (2000). Master's and myth: Little-known information about a popular degree. *Eye on Psi Chi, 4*(2), 19–21, 23, 25.

American Board of Forensic Psychology, & American Psychology-Law Society. (1995). *Petition for the recognition of a specialty in professional psychology.* Retrieved on February 18, 2002, at http://www.unl.edu/ap-ls/petition.PDF

American Psychological Association. (1999). *Employed psychology PhDs by setting: 1997.* Retrieved on August 28, 2003, at http://research.apa.org/doc10.html

American Psychological Association. (2001). *APA Council of Representative Minutes: August 23 and 26, 2001.* Retrieved on July 29, 2002 at http://members.apa.org/governance/council/01aug_minutes.html

American Psychological Association. (2001). *Preparing future faculty program.* Retrieved on January 18, 2002, at http://www.apa.org/ed/pff.html

American Psychological Association. (2002). *APA congressional fellowship program.* Retrieved on August 15, 2002, at http://www.apa.org/ppo/funding/congfell.html

American Psychological Association Practice Directorate. (2002). *Prescriptive authority for psychologists.* Retrieved on July 21, 2004, at http://www.apa.org/apags/profdev/rxpauthority.html

American Psychology-Law Society. (1998). *Careers and training in psychology and law.* Retrieved on March 15, 2002, at http://www.unl.edu/ap-ls/CAREERS.htm

Anson, R. H., & Bloom, M. E. (1988). Police stress in an occupational context. *Journal of Police Science and Administration, 16,* 229–235.

APA Practice Directorate. (2002). *Prescriptive authority for psychologists: An update from APA.* Retrieved on August 22, 2003, at http://www.apa.org/apags/profdev/rxpauthority.html

APA, Division 19. (n.d.). *Introduction to military psychology: An overview.* Retrieved on October 6, 2003, at http://www.apa.org/about/division/div19intro.html

Association of Schools of Public Health. (1994). *What is public health?* Retrieved on September 9, 2003, at http://www.asph.org/document.cfm?page=300

Bartholomew, D. (2001a). Academia or industry: Finding the fit. *Next Wave.* Retrieved on February 1, 2002, at http://nextwave.sciencemag.org/cgi/content/full/2000/08/10/6

Bartholomew, D. (2001b). Academia or industry: Where would I fit in? *Next Wave.* Retrieved on February 1, 2002 at http://nextwave.sciencemag.org/cgi/content/full/2000/06/15/1

Bartol, C. R. (1996). Police psychology then, now, and beyond. *Criminal Justice and Behavior, 23*, 70–89.

Baskin, M. (in press). Public health: Career opportunities for psychologists in public health. In R. M.Morgan, T. L. Kuther, & C. J. Habben (Eds.). *Life after graduate school: Opportunities and advice from new psychologists.* New York: Psychology Press.

Bechtoldt, H., Norcross, J. C., Wyckoff, L. A., Pokrya, M. L., & Campbell, L. F. (2001). Theoretical orientations and employment settings of clinical and counseling psychologists: A comparative study. *The Clinical Psychologist, 54*(1), 3–6.

Bergen, G. T., Aceto, R. T., Chadziewicz, M. M. (1992), Job satisfaction of police psychologists. *Criminal Justice & Behavior Special Issue: Psychology of Policing, 9*(3), 314–329.

Brown, R. T., Freeman, W. S., & Brown, R. A. (2002). The role of psychology in health care delivery. *Professional Psychology: Research & Practice, 33*(6), 536–545.

Bruzzese, J. M. (in press). Medical school and center: The merger of developmental psychology and pediatric asthma education. In R. M. Morgan, T. L. Kuther, & C. J. Habben (Eds.). Life after graduate school: Opportunities and advice from new psychologists. New York: Psychology Press.

Bureau of Labor Statistics. (2002). *Occupational outlook handbook.* Retrieved on October 1, 2003, at http://stats.bls.gov/oco/ocoiab.htm

Careers in the Military. (n.d.). *Psychologists.* Retrieved on October 6, 2003, at http://www.careersinthemilitary.com/index.cfm?fuseaction=search.detail&mc_id=119

Chamberlain, J. (2003). Psychologists shape national policy. *Monitor on Psychology.* Retrieved on September 27, 2004, at http://www. apa.org/monitor/julaug03/shape.html

Christensen, A., & Jacobson, N. S. (1994). Who (or what) can do psychotherapy: The status and challenge of nonprofessional therapies. *Psychological Science, 5*, 8–12.

Chronicle of Higher Education (2003). *Average salaries for full time faculty members,* 2002–2003. Retrieved on October 6, 2003, at http://chronicle.com/prm/weekly/v49/i32/32a01501.htm

Clay, R. (2001). Military psychologists respond to attacks. *Monitor on Psychology.* Retrieved on October 6, 2003, at http://www.apa.org/monitor/nov01/militarypsych.html

Cohen, L., Morgan, R., DeLillo D., & Flores, L. Y. (2003). Why was my major professor so busy? Establishing an academic career while pursuing applied work. *Professional Psychology: Research and Practice, 34*, 88–94.

Copper, C. (1997). An interesting career in psychology: Social science analyst in the public sector. *Psychological Science Agenda.* Retrieved on January 19, 2002, at http://www.apa.org/science/ic–copper.html

Cummings, N. A. (1995). Impact of managed care on employment and training: A primer for survival. *Professional Psychology: Research and Practice, 26*, 10–15.

Davis, K. L. (1997). Emphasizing strengths: Counseling psychologists. In R. J. Sternberg (Ed). *Career paths in psychology: Where your degree can take you.* (pp. 93–116) Washington, DC: American Psychological Association.

Delprino, R. P., Bahn C. (1988). National survey of the extent and nature of psychological services in police departments. *Professional Psychology: Research & Practice, 19*(4), 421–425.

Driskell, J. E., & Olmstead, B. (1989). Psychology and the military: Research applications and trends. *American Psychologist, 44*, 43–54.

Fowler, R. D. (1996). Psychology, public policy, and the congressional fellowship program. In R. P. Lorion, I. Iscoe, P. H. DeLeon, & G. R. VandenBos (Eds.), *Psychology and public policy: Balancing public service and professional need.* (pp. ix–xiv). Washington, DC: American Psychological Association.

Foxhall, K. (2002). More psychologists are attracted to the executive coaching field. *Monitor on Psychology, 33*(4). Retrieved on May 20, 2003, at http://www.apa.org/monitor/apr02/executive.html

Garman, A. N., Whiston, D. L., & Zlatoper, K. W. (2000). Media perceptions of executive coaching and the formal preparation of coaches. *Consulting Psychology Journal: Practice & Research, 52*(3) 201–205.

Gelso, C., & Fretz, B. (2001). *Counseling Psychology* (2nd ed.). Orlando, FL: Harcourt.

Gildewell, J. C., & Livert, D. E. (1992). Confidence in the practice of clinical psychology. *Professional Psychology: Research and Practice, 23*(5), 362–368.

Glasser, J. K. (2002). Factors related to consultant credibility. *Consulting Psychology Journal: Practice and Research, 54*(1), 28–42.

Glassman, J. B. (1998). Preventing and managing board complaints: The downside risk of custody evaluation. *Professional Psychology: Research & Practice, 29*(2), 121–124.

Grodzki, L. (2002). *The new private practice.* New York: Norton.

Habben, C. J. (2003). Obtaining a license to practice psychology. In M. J. Prinstein & M. D. Patterson (Eds.), *The portable mentor: Expert guide to a successful career in psychology.* (pp. 181–190). New York: Kluwer.

Hart, V., Blattner, J., & Leipsic, S. (2001). Coaching verses therapy: A perspective. *Consulting Psychology Journal: Practice and Research, 53*, 229–237.

Hays-Thomas, R. L. (2000). The silent conversation: Talking about the master's degree. *Professional Psychology: Research and Practice, 31*, 339–345.

Herrman, D. (1997). Rewards of public service: Research psychologists in government. In R. J. Sternberg (Ed.), *Career paths in psychology: Where your degree can take you.* (pp. 151–164). Washington, DC: American Psychological Association.

Hersch, L. (1995). Adapting to health care reform and managed care: Three strategies for survival and growth. *Professional Psychology: Research & Practice, 26*, 16–26.

Hess, A. K. (1998). Accepting forensic case referrals: Ethical and professional considerations. *Professional Psychology: Research & Practice, 29*(2), 109–114.

Himelein, M. J. (1999). A student's guide to careers in the helping professions. *Office of Teaching Resources in Psychology.* Retrieved January 3, 2001, from http://www.lemoyne.edu/OTRP/otrpresources/helping.html

Himelein, M. J., & Putnam, E. A. (2001). Work activities of academic clinical psychologists: Do they practice what they teach? *Professional Psychology: Research & Practice, 32*(5), 537–542.

Humphreys, K. (1996). Clinical psychologists as psychotherapists: History, future, and alternatives. *American Psychologist, 51*, 190–197.

Huss, M. T. (2001). What is forensic psychology? It's not *Silence of the Lambs! Eye of Psi Chi, 5*(3), 25–27.

Institute of Medicine, Committee for the Study of the Future of Public Health, Division of Health Care Services (1988). *The future of public health.* Washington, DC: National Academy Press.

Johnson, W. B. (2002). Consulting in the military context. Implications of the revised train-ing principles. *Consulting Psychology Journal: Practice & Research, 54,* 233–241.

Johnson, W. B., & Wilson, K. (1993). The military internship: A retrospective analysis. *Professional Psychology: Research and Practice, 24,* 312–318.

Kampa–Kokesch, & Anderson, M. Z. (2001). Executive coaching: A comprehensive re-view of the literature. *Consulting Psychology Journal: Practice & Research, 53*(4), 205–228

Keith-Spiegel, P., & Wiederman, M. W. (2000). *The complete guide to graduate school ad-mission: Psychology, counseling, and related professions.* Mahwah, NJ: Erlbaum.

Kilburg, R. R. (1996). Toward a conceptual understanding and definition of executive coaching. *Consulting Psychology Journal: Practice and Research, 48,* 134–144.

Kirkland, K., & Kirkland, K. L. (2001). Frequency of child custody evaluation complaints and related disciplinary action: A survey of the Association of State and Provincial Psychology Boards. *Professional Psychology: Research & Practice, 32*(2), 171–174.

Kuther, T. L. (2002). Ethical conflicts in the teaching assignments of graduate students. *Ethics and Behavior, 12,* 197–204.

Kuther, T. L. (2004). *Your career in psychology: Psychology and law.* Pacific Grove, CA: Wadsworth.

Kuther, T. L., & Morgan, R. (2004). *Careers in psychology: Opportunities in a changing world.* Pacific Grove, CA: Wadsworth.

Levant, R. F., Moldawsky, S., & Stigall, T. T. (2000). The evolving profession of psychology: Comment on Hays-Thomas' (2000) "The silent conversation," *Professional Psychol-ogy Research and Practice, 31,* 346–348.

Levant, R.F., Reed, G.M., Ragusea, S.A., DiCowden, M., Murphy, M. J., Sullivan, F., Craig, P.L., & Stout, C. E. (2001). Envisioning and accessing new roles for profes-sional psychology. *Professional Psychology: Research & Practice, 32*(1) 79–87.

Levinson, H. (1996). Executive coaching. *Consulting Psychology Journal: Practice & Re-search, 48*(2) 115–123.

Lloyd, M.A. (2000). *Master's- and doctoral-level careers in psychology and related areas.* Retrieved on February 1, 2000, at http://www.psychwww.com/careers/masters.htm

Lloyd-Bostock, S. (1988). The benefits of legal psychology: Possibilities, practice and dilemmas. *British Journal of Psychology, 79,* 417–440.

Mattas-Curry, L. (1999). Navy to put more psychologists on board. *Monitor on Psychol-ogy.* Retrieved on October 6, 2003, at http://www.apa.org/monitor/julaug99/nl3.html

Max, D. T. (2000, December). The cop and the therapist. *The New York Times Magazine,* p. 94.

National Center for Education Statistics (2003). Postsecondary education. *Digest of Education Sta-tistics, 2002.* Retrieved on August 22, 2003, at http://nces.ed.gov/pubs2003/digest02/ch_3.asp

Nickelson, D. W. (1995). The future of professional psychology in a changing health care marketplace: A conversation with Russ Newman. *Professional Psychology: Research and Practice, 26,* 366–370.

Norcross, J. C. (2000). Clinical vs. counseling psychology: What's the diff? *Eye on Psi Chi, 4*(3), 20–22.

Norcross, J. C., & Castle, P. H. (2002). Appreciating the PsyD: The facts. *Eye on Psi Chi, 7*(1), 22–26.

Norcross, J. C., Prochaska, J. O., & Gallagher, K. M. (1989a). Clinical psychologists in the 1980s: I. Demographics, affiliations, and satisfactions. *The Clinical Psychologist, 42,* 29–39.

Norcross, J. C., Sayette, M. A., Mayne, T. J., Karg, R. S., & Turkson, M. A. (1998). Selecting a doctoral program in professional psychology: Some comparisons among PhD counseling, PhD clinical, and PsyD clinical psychology programs. *Professional Psychology: Research and Practice, 29,* 609–614.

Page, G. D. (1996). Clinical psychology in the military: Developments and issues. *Clinical Psychology Review, 16,* 383–396.

Palmer, C. A., & Baucom, D. H. (1999). Making the most of your clinical Ph.D.: Preparing for a successful career in an evolving and diversified profession. *The Clinical Psychologist, 52,* 7–18.

Parker, L. E., & Detterman, D. K. (1988). The balance between clinical and research interests among Boulder Model graduate students. *Professional Psychology: Research & Practice, 19*(3). 342–344.

Peterson, D. B. (1996). Executive coaching at work: The art of one-on-one change. *Consulting Psychology Journal: Practice & Research, 48*(2) 78–86.

Peterson, D. B., & Hicks, M. D. (1996). *Development FIRST: Strategies for self-development.* Minneapolis, MN: Personnel Decisions International.

Phelps, R., Eisman, E. J., & Kohout, J. (1998). Psychological practice and managed care: Results of the CAPP practitioner survey. *Professional Psychology: Research and Practice, 29,* 31–36.

Preparing Future Faculty. (n.d.). *Preparing future faculty.* Retrieved on January 18, 2002, at http://www.preparing faculty.org/PFFWeb.Resources.htm

Rabaska, L. (2000). More psychologists in the trenches. *Monitor on Psychology.* Retrieved on October 6, 2003, at http://www.apa.org/monitor/jun00/trenches.html

Roediger, H. (1997). Teaching, research, and more: Psychologists in an academic career. In R. J. Sternberg (Ed.), *Career paths in psychology: Where your degree can take you* (pp. 7–30). Washington, DC: American Psychological Association.

Salzinger, K. (1995). The academic life. *Psychological Science Agenda.* Retrieved on January 18, 2002, at http://www.apa.org/psa/janfeb95/acad.html

Scrivner, E. M., & Kurke, M. I. (1995). Police psychology at the dawn of the 21st century. In M. I. Kurke & E. M. Scrivner (Eds.), *Police psychology into the 21st century* (pp. 3–30). Hillsdale, NJ: Erlbaum.

Seligman, M. E. P. (1995). The effectiveness of psychotherapy: The Consumer Reports Study. *American Psychologist, 50,* 965–974.

Selkin, J. (1994). Psychological autopsy: Scientific psychohistory or clinical intuition? *American Psychologist, 49,* 74–75.

Shneidman, E. S. (1994). The psychological autopsy. *American Psychologist, 49,* 75–76.

Sierles, F. S. & Taylor, M. A. (1995). Decline of U.S. medical student career choice of psychiatry and what to do about it. *American Journal of Psychiatry, 152,* 1416–1426.

Simon, E. P., & Folen, R. A. (2001). The role of the psychologist on the multidisciplinary pain management team. *Professional Psychology: Research & Practice, 32*(2), 125–134.

Singleton, D., Tate, A., & Randall, G. (2003). *Salaries in Psychology 2001: Report of the 2001 APA Salary Survey.* Retrieved on October 6, 2003, at http://research.apa.org/01salary/index.html

Smith, D. (2002). Taking it to the fleet. *Monitor on Psychology.* Retrieved on October 6, 2003, at http://www.apa.org/monitor/nov02/fleet.html

Society of Clinical Psychology. (2002). *What is clinical psychology?* Retrieved August, 22, 2003, at http://www.apa.org/divisions/div12/aboutcp.html

Somerville, K. (1998). Where is the business of business psychology headed? *Consulting Psychology Journal: Practice & Research, 50*(4) 237–241.

Souter, C. (2002). Military psychologists encounter unique work challenges. *Masspsy.com*. Retrieved on October 6, 2003, at http://www.masspsy.com/leading/0202_covermilitary.html

Stein, D. M., & Lambert, M. J. (1995). On the relationship between therapist experience and psychotherapy outcome. *Journal of Consulting and Clinical Psychology, 63,* 182–196.

Super, J. T. (1999). Forensic psychology and law enforcement. In A. K. Hess, & I. B. Weiner (Eds.), *The handbook of forensic psychology* (pp. 409–439). New York: Wiley.

Susman-Stillman, A. R., Brown, J. L., Adam, E. K., Blair, C., Gaines, R., Gordon, R. A. et al. (1996). Building research and policy connections: Training and career options for developmental scientists. *Social Policy Report, 10*(4), 1–19.

Tremper, C. R. (1987). Organized psychology's efforts to influence judicial policy-making. *American Psychologist, 42*(5), 496–501.

Trull, T. J., & Phares, E. J. (2001). *Clinical psychology.* Belmont, CA: Wadsworth/Thomson Learning.

Vesilind, P. A. (2000). *So you want to be a professor? A handbook for graduate students.* Thousand Oaks, CA: Sage.

Vincent, T. A. (1990). A view from the Hill: The human element in policy making on Capitol Hill. *American Psychologist, 45*(1), 61–64.

Walker, L. E. (1990). Psychological assessment of sexually abused children for legal evaluation and expert witness testimony. *Professional Psychology: Research & Practice, 21*(5), 344–353.

Williams, C. (2000). *Prescription privileges fact sheet: What students should know about the APA's pursuit of prescription privileges for psychologists (RxP).* Retrieved on August 22, 2003, at http://www.apa.org/apags/profdev/prespriv.html

Williams, S., Wicherski, M., & Kohout, J. L. (2000). *Salaries in psychology 1999: Report of the 1999 APA salary survey.* Washington, DC: American Psychological Association. Retrieved on June 5, 2002, at http://research.apa.org/99salaries.html

Wiskoff, M. F. (1997). Defense of the nation: Military psychologists. In R. J. Sternberg (Ed.), *Career paths in psychology: Where your degree can take you* (pp. 245–268). Washington, DC: American Psychological Association.

Witherspoon, R. & White, R. P. (1996). Executive coaching: A continuum of roles. *Consulting Psychology Journal: Practice and Research, 48,* 124–133.

Wrightsman, L. S. (2001). *Forensic psychology.* Belmont, CA: Wadsworth.

Wrightsman, L. S., Greene, E., Neitzel, M. T., & Fortune, W. H. (2002). *Psychology and the Legal System.* Belmont, CA: Wadsworth.

Young, J., & Weishaar, M. E. (1997). Psychologists in private practice. In R. J. Sternberg (Ed.), *Career paths in psychology: Where your degree can take you* (pp. 71–92). Washington, DC: American Psychological Association.

Index

A

Academic careers, 97–101
    activities in, 98–100
    advantages and disadvantages in, 100–102
    clinical practice and, 100
    competitiveness of job market, 101
    McFall, Richard M., profile of, 106–108
    preparation for, 104–105
    public health research psychologists, 36
    research and, 99, 102–103
    salaries in, 101
    service responsibilities, 99–100
    teaching responsibilities, 99
Academic freedom, 100
Aceto, R. T., 69
Activities of practicing psychologists, 14–15
Actkinson, T. R., 5, 98
Adjudicative competence, 65
Advantages of psychology career, 16–17
AIDS projects, 48
Aircraft carriers, psychologists on, 54
Alcohol and drug abuse counselors, 5–6
American Association for the Advancement of Science: Policy Fellowships, 38
American Board of Forensic Psychology, 64
American Cancer Society, 35
American Enterprise Institute, 36
American Psychological Association, 52, 55, 64, 67, 68, 98
    amicus curiae briefs for, 35–36
    Congressional Fellowship Program, 37–38, 45–49
    licensure requirements, 118–119
    Preparing Future Faculty, 105
    prescriptive authority issue, 7
American Psychology-Law Society, 64, 67
Amicus curiae briefs, 35–36
Analyze This, 2

Anderson, M. Z., 85
Anson, R. H., 69
Anti-spam legislation, 46–47
Applied experience, obtaining, 120
Assessment, 14
Association of Schools of Public Health, 34
Autopsies, psychological, 66–67
Awakening to Midlife, 2

B

Bahn, C., 68
Bartholomew, D., 102, 103
Bartol, C. R., 68, 69, 70
Baskin, Monica L., 35
    profile of, 42–45
Baucom, D. H., 18
Bechtoldt, H., 4
Bergen, G. T., 69, 70
Berry, Marilu Price, profile of, 27–29
Bethesda Naval Hospital, 57
Billing activities, 15
Bingaman, Jeff, 46
Blattner, J., 85
Bloom, M. E., 69
Bootzin, R. R., 100
Boulder Model, 109, 116
Brooke Army Medical Center: Clinical Psychology Residence Program, 57
The Brookings Institution, 36
Brotman, Lloyd, 93, 94
Brown, R. A., 16
Brown, R. T., 16
Bruzzese, J. M., 39
Budman, Simon H., profile of, 40–42
Bureau of Labor Statistics, 5, 56
Butters, Charles, 109

C

Campbell, L. F., 4
Career counselors, 5–6
Careers in the Military, 52

Castle, P. H., 116
Catherine Acuff Congressional Fellow-
ship, 38
Center for Creative Leadership, 94
Center for Health Care Strategies, 36
Center for Studying Health System
Change, 36
Centers for Disease Control and Preven-
tion, 35
Chadziewicz, M. M., 69
Chamberlain, J., 49
Child abuse allegations, 65
Child custody evaluations, 66
ethical issues in, 67
Children's Defense Fund, 36
Christensen, A., 114
Civil cases, forensic psychologists in,
66–67
Clay, R., 55
Clinical psychology, 2–3
counseling psychology differenti-
ated, 4
doctoral degrees in, 115–118
Heiby, Elaine M., profile of, 9–11
master's degrees in, 114–115
Clinical supervision, 14–15
Clinician-scientist training model, 115
Cognitive behavioral orientation, 14
Colleges
meeting with professors, 120
Colleges and universities. *See also* Aca-
demic careers
counseling centers, working in, 16
Communication skills, 18
Community colleges, careers in, 98
Community mental health centers, 16
Competence issues
in civil cases, 66
in criminal cases, 65
Comprehensive exams, 117
Congress, psychologists in, 37–38
Congressional Gift of Life Medal, 48
Consulting careers, 81–96. *See also* Man-
agement consultants
Copper, C., 103, 104
Counseling psychology, 3
clinical psychology differentiated, 4
doctoral degrees in, 115–118
master's degrees in, 114–115
Counselors, 5–6

Cozzarelli, Cathy, 46
Criminal cases, forensic psychologists in, 65
CSI, 64
Cummings, N. A., 6

D
Davis, K. L., 16
Delprino, R. P., 68
Demaine, Linda, 46–47
Department of Defense, 47
Department of Energy, 47
Detterman, D. K., 14
Developing countries, working for, 48–49
Disadvantages of psychology career,
16–17
Dissertations, 117–118
Doctoral degrees, 115–118
post-doctoral specialization, 118
requirements for, 117–118
training models, 115–116
Dorson, Carrie, profile of, 59–61
Dr. Phil, 2
Driskell, J. E., 5

E
Eisenhower Army Medical Center: Clinical
Psychology Residency Training, 57
Eisman, E. J., 6
Emergency room centers, 16
Emotional Intelligence at Work, 2
Employment settings, 15–16
for public health careers, 35
Ethics
forensic psychology issues, 67
licensure and, 119
military careers and, 55
Examination for Professional Practice in
Psychology (EPPP), 119
Executive coaches, 84–87
activities of, 84–85
advantages and disadvantages of careers, 85–86
contexts for, 85
focus of work, 92
preparation for career as, 86–87
regulation of field, 86
salaries of, 85
sampling field, 94–95
Shullman, Sandra on, 91–95
Executive search consultants, 82

Exner, John, 106
Experience, acquiring, 120
Expert testimony, 35
    by forensic psychologists, 67

F
Families and Work Institute, 36
FBI (Federal Bureau of Investigation), 46–47
Fee-for-service mental health care, 6
Fellowship Training Program, 57
Financial management classes, 18
Folen, R. A., 16, 17
Forensic psychology, 64–68
    activities in, 65–67
    advantages and disadvantages of careers in, 67
    Franklin, Karen, profile of, 72–74
    Nelson, Evan, profile of, 74
    preparing for career in, 68
For-profit organizations and public health, 35
Fowler, R. D., 34, 37
Foxhall, K., 84, 86, 87, 91–95
Franklin, Karen, profile of, 72–74
Freeman, W. S., 16
Fretz, B., 4, 14, 15
Fringe benefits, 17
Frivolous lawsuits, 67

G
Garman, A. N., 84, 86
Gelso, C., 4, 14, 15
Gildewell, J. C., 17
The Glass Ceiling: Can Women Reach the Top of America's Largest Corporations? (White), 92
Glasser, J. K., 87
Glassman, J. B., 67
Globalization and executive coaching, 92
Government, research careers in, 103–104
Graduate degrees. See also Doctoral degrees; Master's degrees
    preparation for, 121
Grant-writing, 36
Grodzki, L., 85
Group practices, 15
Guidance counselors, 5–6

H
Habben, C. J., 118, 119

Harris, Lauren Julius, 109
Hart, V., 85, 86
Hays-Thomas, R. L., 114
Health care system. *See also* Managed care; Public health careers
    policy careers, 47–48
    and private practice, 15
Health education programs, 35
Heiby, Elaine M., profile of, 9–11
Hersch, L., 6
Hess, A. K., 67
Hicks, M. D., 84
Himelein, M. J., 7, 14, 15
Hospital centers, 16
Hostage Negotiation Teams (HNT), eligibility for, 69
Humphreys, K., 6, 7
Huss, M. T., 65, 77

I
Industry, research careers in, 103
Information technology consultants, 82
Institute of Medicine, 34
Insurance companies. *See also* Managed care
    and private practice, 15
Internship programs, 120
Issues in psychology, 6–7

J
Jackson, Tamara, 47
Jacobson, N. S., 114
Johnson, W. B., 52, 55, 56, 57
Johnstone, Brick, profile of, 19–22

K
Kampa-Kokesch, S., 85
Kaufmann, Gary, profile of, 78–79
Keith-Spiegel, P., 4
Kilburg, R. R., 84
Kirchman, Ellen, profile of, 77–78
Kirkland, K., 67
Kirkland, K. L., 67
Kirschner, Neil, 45, 47–48
Kohout, J. L., 6, 37
Kralj, Mary, 93
Kurke, M. I., 68
Kuther, T. L., 35, 64, 67, 70, 105, 119

L
Lambert, M. J., 114

Leadership, military careers and, 53
Leahy, Patrick, 46
Legal system. See Forensic psychology
Leipsic, S., 85
Levant, R. F., 34, 114
Levinson, H., 85
Licensure, 118–119
Listening skills, 18
Livert, D. E., 17
Lloyd, M. A., 98, 104, 115
Lloyd-Bostock, S., 67
Lobbying, 35
Lowman, Rodney, 92–93

M
Malingering, 65
Managed care, 6
      learning about, 18
      policy careers and, 49
Management consultants, 82–84
      advantages and disadvantages of ca-
      reers, 83
      preparing for career, 84–85
      salaries for, 83
      William, Steven, profile of, 88–91
Manpower Demonstration Research Cor-
      poration, 36
Marginalization of psychologists, 6
Marketing classes, 18
Master's degrees, 114–115
MSW (master's in social work), 5
      requirements for obtaining, 115
Math education, 47
Mattas-Curry, L., 54
Max, D. T., 68
McFall, Richard M., profile of, 106–108
Medical centers, 16
Medicare, 48
Military careers, 51–61
      activities of, 52–54
      advantages and disadvantages of,
      54–56
      direct counseling services, 53–54
      Dorson, Carrie, profile of, 59–61
      ethical issues and, 55
      housing allowance, 56
      leadership and team work in, 53
      personal goals and, 58
      preparation for, 56–58
      resources for, 57

salaries, 55–56
selection/classification of personnel, 52
      training of personnel, 52–53
Modawsky, S., 114
Morgan, R., 35, 70, 119
MSW (master's in social work), 5

N
NASA, 47
National Board of Certified Counselors
      and Affiliates Web site, 6
National Center for Education Statistics,
      2, 3
National Center for Policy Analysis, 36
National Institute on Drug Abuse, 35
National Institutes of Mental Health, 35
National Science and Technology Council,
      47
Nelson, Evan, profile of, 74–76
New Mexico, prescriptive authority in, 7
Nickelson, D. W., 6
Nonprofit organizations
      public health careers and, 35, 36
      research careers in, 104
Norcross, J. C., 4, 116, 117
NSF (National Science Foundation), 47

O
Office of Science and Technology Policy
      (OSTP), 47
Olmstead, B., 52
One-on-one work with clients, 14
Operations management consultants, 82
Oprah, 2
Organ donors, 48
Organizational development consultants, 82

P
Page, G. D., 52
Palmer, C. A., 18
Parker, L. E., 14
Peltier, Bruce, 93
Peterson, D. B., 84, 85
Phares, E. J., 4, 6, 12, 14, 15, 106–108
Ph.D. programs, 116–117
      dissertations, 117–118
Phelps, R., 6
Pokrywa, M. L., 4
Police psychology, 68–70
      activities in, 68–69

advantages and disadvantages of careers in, 69–70
fitness for duty determinations, 69
Kaufmann, Gary, profile of, 78–79
Kirchman, Ellen, profile of, 77–78
operational and organizational support, 69
preparing for careers in, 70
salaries in, 70
selection of officers, 68
training police officers, 69
Policy-related organizations, 35
Politics and psychologists, 37–38
Post-doctoral specialization, 118
Practice Organization's Health Policy Fellowship, 45
Practicing psychologists, activities of, 14–15
Preparing Future Faculty, 105
Prescriptive authority, 7
Private practice, 15
advantages and disadvantages of, 17
forensic psychologists in, 67
preparing for, 18
Professional psychologist-practitioner training model, 115
Professors. See also Academic careers
meeting with, 120
Profiler, 64
Profiles
Barry, Marilu Price, 27–29
Baskin, Monica L., 42–45
Budman, Simon H., 40–42
Dorson, Carrie, 59–61
Franklin, Karen, 72–74
Heiby, Elaine M., 9–11
Johnstone, Brick, 19–22
Kaufmann, Gary, 77–78
Kirchman, Ellen, 77–78
McFall, Richard M., 106–108
Nelson, Evan, 74
Shullman, Sandra, 91–95
Snider, Brian, 30–31
Snyder, Peter J., 109–111
Tentoni, Stuart, 22–27
Williams, Steven, 88–91
Program development and evaluation careers, 38–39
Psychiatrists, 5
Psychological autopsies, 66–67
Psychological damages, 66

Psychological Science Agenda, 111
The Psychology of Executive Coaching (Peltier), 93
Psychotherapy groups, 14
Psy.D programs, 116–117
dissertations, 117–118
Public health careers
amicus curiae briefs, 35–36
career tracks in, 35–39
defined, 34
preparation for, 39
program development and evaluation careers, 38–39
research careers in, 35–37
Public policy fellowship programs, 37–38
Publishing and academic careers, 100–101
Putnam, E. A., 14

R
Rabaska, L., 54
RAND, 36
Randall, G., 17, 83
Rangel, Charles B., 48
Research
academic careers and, 99, 102–103
careers in, 102–105
counseling psychologists in, 3
experience, obtaining, 120
government, research careers in, 103–104
industry, careers in, 103
nonprofit organizations, careers in, 104
policy-related research, 35–37
preparation for careers in, 104–105
program development and evaluation careers, 38–39
public health careers and, 35–37
salaries in research careers, 102
Snyder, Peter J., profile of, 109–111
social service agency careers, 104
training in, 18
Research Triangle Institute, 35
Ricki Lake, 2
Roediger, H., 99, 101

S
Salaries
in academic careers, 101
for executive coaches, 85

in forensic psychology, 67
for management consultants, 83
in military careers, 55–56
of police psychologists, 70
in research careers, 102
table of, 17
Salzinger, K., 101
Scholar-practitioner model, 116
Science education, 47
Science Policy Fellowship Program, 45
Scientist-practitioner training model, 115
Scrivner, E. M., 68
Seligman, M. E. P., 114
Selkin, J., 67
Shneidman, E. S., 66–67
Shullman, Sandra, 91–95
Silence of the Lambs, 64
Simon, E. P., 16, 17
Singleton, D., 17, 83
Smith, D., 53
Snider, Brian, profile of, 30–31
Snyder, Peter J., profile of, 109–111
Social policy careers, 34
preparation for, 39
Social service research careers, 104
Social workers, 5
Society for Industrial and Organizational
Society, 94
Society for Research in Child Develop-
ment: Congressional and Executive
Branch Fellowships, 38
Society of Clinical Psychology, 2
Society of Consulting Psychology, 94
Somerville, K., 87
Souter, C., 54, 56
Spam, battling, 46–47
Stein, D. M., 114
Stigall, T. T., 114
Strategic management consultants, 82
Stress, 17
military psychologists and, 54
police psychologists and, 69, 70
Substance Abuse and Mental Health Ser-
vices Administration (SAMHSA),
48, 49
Super, J. T., 68, 79
Survival Evasion Resistance Escape
(SERE) training, 53
Susman-Stillman, A.R., 39
SWAT teams, eligibility for, 69

T
Tate, A., 17, 83
Tentoni, Stuart, profile of, 22–27
Tenure in academic careers, 100
Therapeutic skills, 18
Think-tank organizations, 35–36
Thompson, Mischa, 48–49
Tippins, Nancy, 93–94
Tremper, C. R., 36
Tripler Army Medical Center programs, 57
Trull, T. J., 4, 6, 12, 14, 15, 106–108

U
Universities. *See also* Academic careers
counseling centers, working in, 16
meeting with professors, 120
U.S. Army Clinical Psychology Residency
Programs, 57
U.S. Navy, Clinical Psychology Internship
Program of, 57

V
V.A. facilities, 16
Vail model, 116
Vesilind, P. A., 98, 100
Victim trauma and injury, 65
Vincent, T. A., 37

W
Walker, L. E., 65
Wallace, William, 49
Walter Reed Army Medical Center: Psy-
chology Training Programs, 57
Wasylyshyn, Karol M., 92, 95
Web sites
military career resources, 57
National Board of Certified Coun-
selors and Affiliates, 6
policy-related organizations, 36
Preparing Future Faculty, 105
public policy fellowship programs, 38
think tank organizations, 36
Weishaar, M. E., 14, 15
Welfare reauthorization, 46
What About Bob?, 2
Whiston, D. L., 84
White, Randall P., 84, 92
White House Fellows Program, 38
Wicherski, M., 37
Wiederman, M. W., 4

Willford Hall Medical Center: Clinical
    Psychology Residence (Internship)
    Program, 57
William A. Bailey AIDS Policy Congres-
    sional Fellowship, 38
Williams, C., 7
Williams, S., 37
Williams, Steven, profile of, 88–91
Wilson, K., 56, 57
Wiskoff, M. F., 52, 55, 56

Witherspoon, R., 84
Wrightsman, L. S., 35, 64, 65, 69
Wyckoff, L. A., 4

Y
Young, J., 14, 15

Z
Zlatoper, K. W., 84